Advance Praise for
Better Leaders, Better Teams

Every manager seeks to generate success in the workplace. Yet human beings are complicated, unique, and demand consistent, respectful attention. Meet this challenge by using any chapter of this book that offers an integrated view of the science of human development, the practices for creating healthy team dynamics and actions, and the art of being human with each other, no matter what. The combination of consultative process approaches with the amplifying power of coaching to maximize both individual and team potential provides leaders, team members, and coach practitioners with a rich toolbox to drive desired outcomes.

—Janet M. Harvey, CEO inviteCHANGE, ICF Master Certified Coach, Best-Selling Author, *Invite Change*

Sami Bugay has crafted a clear, well-organized, and impeccably written guide. *Better Leaders, Better Teams* serves as both a training manual and a valuable reference. As a longtime coach and trainer, I particularly appreciate the fresh approach he takes integrating numerous models of human awareness and interaction that will open new possibilities for any team leader, individual member, or coach. Sami generously shares insights from his learning experiences that make his teachings personal and relevant. Highly recommended!

—Dan Newby, author of *The Unopened Gift: A Primer in Emotional Literacy* and founder of www.schoolofemotions.world

It is not often that we come across a person who is willing to ponder difficult questions and submit himself to truly understand the entire range of human experience. Sami Bugay is such a man. With courage and conviction he has traveled between science and art to find the most powerful elements that illuminate our human story. *Better Leaders, Better Teams* is a practical guide that integrates many valuable elements of his research and personal discovery and offers readers an opportunity to engage in a playful and introspective manner to more deeply understand themselves and the teams they belong to.

—Kimberly Hunn, MCC, Founder of Edgewalker Group International (EGI), www.edgewalkergroup.com

I appreciate the book's conversational practical language for ease of understanding and implementation. Bravo, and well done!

—Amoráh Ross, ICF Master Certified Coach | Certified Mentor Coach | Certified Professional Coach

BETTER LEADERS BETTER TEAMS

A Ready-to-Use Combination of Grounded Theory and
Experiential Practice to Build Fully Functional Teams

SAMI BUGAY

MCC - Master Certified Coach – ICF
NCC - Certified Ontological Coach
PCC Assessor & Mentor – ICF

First of all, I want to express my sincere gratitude to my dad Ali Bugay and my mom Firuzan Bugay, my brother Selçuk Bugay, my son Erim Bugay, who is mentioned in all my works, all of the teachers who came into my life and taught me so much that I may or may not even be aware of, and my colleague Özlem Erten, who encouraged me, supported me, and labored with me to see this book become a reality.

Thank you!
Sami Bugay

Contents

Foreword
by Dr. Martin Egan

It is rare to find a handbook for developing teams that both the team member and the coach can use. Sami Bugay writes from his experience as a corporate team member and employee as well as a team coach and consultant in organizations. His grasp of individual and team psychology is masterful and shows in the exercises he's developed. The book offers a holistic, informed perspective with a systemic approach to team coaching.

The simple, straightforward, ready-to-go exercises set out in the book provide tools for any team member on topics such as getting to know each other better, using metaphors and coaching exercises, getting agreements, and team alignment. Even when a coach isn't available, individual team members can do quite a bit of work by following the exercises set out in each chapter.

For the team coach, the book contains novel approaches to typology, and understanding team archetypes with questionnaires for self-assessment.

This is a story of teams in the context of their environment and in their organization. Bugay addresses the complex dynamics of a person's inner world, the interpersonal relationships, the group and the organization and how they relate to each other.

Ken Wilber's Integral approach is made very practical and accessible throughout. This especially shows with the activity on identifying personal and team values, as well as the suggestions for overcoming obstacles and working with teams in transition. There's even an insightful activity on expressing emotions and how body language affects the expression of emotion. For those who want to go into deeper developmental work, there's a shadow exercise to increase awareness of the shadow behaviors that might affect us in teams.

Bugay's book integrates Jungian and integral thinking with practical performance psychology for any team.

—Dr. Martin Egan, Psychotherapist/Organizational consultant

Preface

Life is a team sport

The fact that you are reading this book probably means that you are the leader or a member of a team, or that we are colleagues who work with teams. First of all, I want to congratulate you for striving to improve your knowledge and skills even further. Thank you for not being content with where you are now, for desiring to go further, doing the necessary research, and for choosing my book. I had only one motive in writing this book. I wanted to save you the trouble I experienced in my over 30-year career by sharing what I've learned and by supporting you in your efforts to better yourself.

If you were born in Turkey in the 1970s, your childhood memories will include waiting in line to buy margarine and cigarettes for your parents, and if your family had a car, you will remember waiting in long lines with your dad for gasoline. You will remember the fighting between the left and the right in your high school and university years, the esteemed intellectuals that lost their lives merely for having a different opinion, and dealing with average inflation of 70%—sometimes more than 100%—when you started your career. You will also remember a country where it was actually illegal to possess foreign currency, where economic crises happened every five years, where there were curfews and military coups. These were the circumstances under which I began my career. I grew up afraid for my life and in love with learning.

My first encounter with team sports was the soccer matches we played in the alley. All of us kids took turns being the team captain. Every weekend that it didn't snow in Istanbul, no matter how cold it was, I was playing a game of soccer where each captain flipped a coin to start choosing their team. This was when I first began to understand that choosing the best players was not all it took to win, that winning required much more than this, and that sometimes you had to let go of the best players for the good of the team if you wanted to win.

After I graduated with a degree in Mathematics Engineering from Istanbul Technical University, my job consisted mostly of a monotonous life sitting in front of a keyboard and a monitor. One day one of my quieter colleagues said, "Sami, take a look at this code I have written. It is constantly giving me a compilation error. I have been trying to fix it all day without any success." These words woke me from my slumber. This was the first time I realized that a second pair of eyes could be tremendously valuable. I understood that my mistakes could be more easily understood by someone on the outside, and that finding a companion that I could trust in this regard would be instructive, invaluable, and a dynamic that would lead to joint success.

I began my professional career as a computer programmer and worked my way up through various management positions until I was finally the assistant general manager of an e-commerce company. This was when another economic crisis brought me to a vastly different place. About ten days after a 100% currency devaluation, the general manager called me to his office and told me that we had to merge with one of the group companies, and that a lot of people would be laid off from both companies. I was forced to handle a process that is extremely difficult for a manager. It was a heartbreaking and challenging process to lay off so many colleagues that I had worked shoulder-to-shoulder with up until then as well as many employees from the sister company that I was hardly familiar with, and then to create a team from the people that were left. It was no easy task to motivate myself and those who were left after the dust settled from all the carnage, and then to win their trust and make them believe in a new goal.

When I look back on those days now, I know that if I had had the experience I have gained working with managers and teams at different levels, and if I had known the approaches that I have put together over the last ten years, I would have been able to oversee a much healthier, effective, and more pleasant transition. I still bear the pain of that time deep in my heart.

It is my earnest hope that the book you hold in your hands will give you ideas, approaches, and insights that will help you overcome the difficulties you face.

I wish you every success.

Sami Bugay
MCC – Master Certified Coach - ICF
NCC – Certified Ontological Coach
PCC Assessor & Mentor Coach - ICF

Why Teams?

Actually, any manager who has given years of their life to the corporate world knows the answer to this question: The results that we achieve together are much more valuable, much more creative, and much greater than anything we could come up with on our own.

I have worked in organizations where goals were set by senior management, or even imposed on subordinates from abroad in multinational companies; where common objectives were only perceived as numerical values; where feedback was often not provided in order to maintain good relations, and when it was given, human resources or senior management were made to bear responsibility for it; where the hallway gossip mill ran continuously; where everyone claimed to trust each other, but their actions demonstrated the exact opposite; where everyone agreed on the solutions, but after the meeting was over, every person who attended did what they thought was best in their own departments; where communication was two steps forward and one step back and sometimes completely toxic; where lethargy often reigned and everyone's habit was to hold others responsible instead of being responsible themselves. In fact, I have sometimes done these very things myself, whether intentionally or not. If you have experienced several or all of the difficulties I just listed, the approaches outlined in this book are just what your team or organization needs! You are holding a book that may not answer all of your questions but will provide solutions for many of them on different levels.

How Can You Use This Book?

If You Are A Manager:

If you ever ate honeysuckle when you were a child, you know that you have to suck a ton of flowers to get enough of that drop of delectable sweetness. For me, the same thing applied to much of the training I received in my corporate career. There was a ton of dogma about what was necessary and what had to be avoided, but the sweet nectar of truth was hard to come by.

Research conducted by Harvard, one of the world's leading universities, supports this argument. Only 2% of the information shared by an instructor in an adult learning environment will remain as changed behavior after one year. However, this figure has been shown to rise as high as 40% with coaching and experiential learning.

Therefore, if you are a manager, you can observe the needs of your team and step-by-step you can build a bridge to the goals you want to reach with the help of this book. Not only will you be helping your team members with their individual success, but you will also be making collective success and unity possible.

You can make success sustainable by unleashing the team's ability, competency, and resources, ensuring that potential energy is transformed into kinetic energy, and if necessary, pooling resources and directing them to the team member that needs them while fostering loyalty and a sense of belonging on the team to ensure a peaceful work environment even in the most difficult times.

If You Are A Team Member:

Life itself is entirely a team sport. It is impossible for us to survive in this world on our own, and I need "you" in order to define who "I" am. All of us impute meaning to the events and situations we encounter. After a while, however, the only thing we remember is the meaning we gave it and not the event or situation. For example, if our company becomes less profitable or sales decline, we interpret this as a need for more marketing or new sales activities, or we might say that we need better training. The meaning that we give to the event determines our actions, but sometimes the results we get from the actions we take are not satisfactory and do not make us happy. We want different results.

This is when we start trying different approaches, some of which are effective and some of which are not. We find ourselves in the same suboptimal cycle. Ken Wilber is a contemporary philosopher and thinker with a systems perspective. He says that we don't need different maps. Instead, we need to transform those who make the maps.

It is the members of the team that shape its achievements and blaze a trail to achieving its objectives. In this book, you will find definitions that will help you describe that nameless block that you have observed in yourself or on your team and which you realize is still an obstacle to your progress. You will also find practices that will help you overcome this block.

If You Are A Facilitator Or Coach Who Works With Teams:

As your colleague, there is something I want to share from my heart. The book you hold in your hand offers a number of perspectives, approaches, and practices that can make a difference within teams and leaders you support, and provides both the theory and the practice to make sure that they clearly understand and experience this difference. You will knead into this dough your own competency, capacity, interpretation, and star dust to create delicacies for every audience you address and every setting you work in.

1 MANAGEMENT, COACHING, AND LEADERSHIP

Systemic Approach and Team Coaching

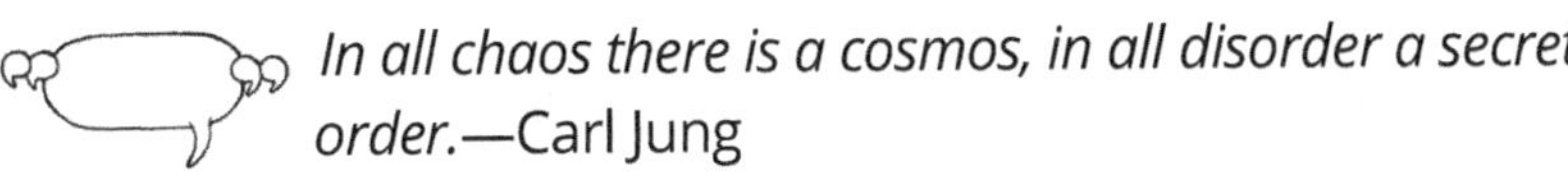 *In all chaos there is a cosmos, in all disorder a secret order.* —Carl Jung

When we look at consulting approaches over the last 30 years, we see that they are focused on human nature and the different parts of the systems people find themselves in.

The work-personal life balance, skill management, goal setting, achieving goals, and similar outcome-focused approaches are the processes that support individual, team and organizational development and awareness.

All of these approaches not only reveal our identity and values both as individuals and organizations, but they move us one step further on our journey. They seem valuable and effective. However, new methods that can take the system even further than the collective balance it has achieved make it possible for us to look at the issues we encounter from a much broader perspective so that we can make an even greater contribution to the whole.

When I refer to a systemic approach, I am not referring to an organization's paper hierarchy or its vision, mission, values, culture, or workplace conditions. I am talking about merging an approach that combines the wisdom we possess with mind, heart, and spirit on every level.

From this point forward, we will examine the fundamental concepts of Systemic/Organizational Coaching and look at their role in this approach and their importance.

Global View of Systems

Today, there are many approaches to consultancy. Some are individual, others are facilitation, and some are conducted for teams and groups. We see models built around goal setting, team building or leadership skills development, and emotional intelligence.

However, in my work as a coach or consultant, what I observe in the managers, leaders, and employees working at different levels in companies—i.e., the ways in which the dynamics deep inside the organization or individual systems manifest themselves—is "coerced behavior," pressure, teams that have lost their effectiveness, an inability to adapt to the different roles required by career and personal life, vicious cycles, conflict, and broken relationships between people. These situations have a negative effect on both the individual and the team or organization that they are a part of.

Chaos, Order, and Harmony

In 1961, Edward Lorenz conducted the experiment that resulted in what is known today as the "butterfly effect." Lorenz was performing weather forecasts and working on a model that included a lengthy series of computer calculations, which took a long time to complete. Instead of redoing the calculations, he wanted to repeat the test using the numerical results he had just obtained, and he conducted the test again entering the previous inputs into the system. When he looked at the printouts, the results were shocking. The new results bore no similarity to the previous data. However, the new results should have been practically the same as the previous results. As he was thinking over these unexpected results, he realized that he had made some insignificant rounding to the figures that were entered into the computer.

In principle, such insignificant rounding should have had no effect on the results, but it did.

Based on this experiment, Lorenz concluded that long-range weather forecasts were impossible. He had come face to face with the fact that even very small changes in weather conditions that occur on any given day could have a dramatic effect on forecasts just a few weeks out, and that these tiny changes were unpredictable. Even though this experiment by Lorenz was unexpected, it would lay the foundations for the new principle of chaos theory.

In 1992, Chris Langton from the Santa Fe Institute came up with the following equation:

Order -> Complexity -> Chaos

The arrows in the equation denote the transition from one state to the other. According to Langton, complexity is the turning point and the balance between order and chaos. Gregoire Nicolis and Ilya Prigogine enriched the thesis by adding that complexity represents the transition of the system between different models of behavior under different conditions.

According to Jung, the process of identity formation and maturation is the result of a series of internal psychological processes (Jung, 1959). These processes are "complex and difficult … and in this respect are comparable to all other biological processes." Jung was keenly aware of the fact that order comes from chaos.

The chaos in our lives helps us experience a transformation through a psychological process and transition to a universal order.

Chaos and order are like the two extremes of a pendulum; every system, whether it is individuals, teams, or organizations, fluctuates back and forth between these two extremes. Without chaos, it is impossible to have creativity, change, transformation, flow, movement, energy, and momentum. Without order, it is impossible to have balance, stability, clarity, tranquility, control, sustainability, and certainty. In those times and areas where we feel relatively chaotic, there is something that the system, whether individual, team, or organization, is trying to draw to our attention. The system sounds the alarm regularly and persistently.

When we pay attention and take the time to understand the sound and what it means and then devote some space to this in our life, the truth starts to rise up from the murky depths to the surface. Just like bubbles rising from deep under the water create a kind of chaos and turbidity, when you let go of what you are holding inside, it creates turbulence and discomfort, but when this is past, the water becomes clear and calm.

When the facts and dynamics in any system are ignored, they result in turbulence, discomfort, blockage, bloating, constant difficulty, and other similar feelings that negatively affect performance.

 *Every part is a representative of the whole.*
—Anonymous

And as long as each part belongs to the whole, any change to a part changes the whole.

The History of Coaching

Coach is an old French word for "a vehicle that transports people from one place to another." It began to be used similarly in English in the 1500s.

Later, in the 1840s, it was used for special instructors who prepared students for the exam at Oxford University. After 1889, the word *coach* began to be used in the more modern meaning for individuals who trained teams of athletes. The contemporary meaning of the term coach was used by Dr. Dick Borough in 1985 to describe his own style of leadership. It is striking that the definition of coaching became more mainstream after a *Forbes* magazine article entitled "Sigmund Freud versus Henry Ford," published in 1988.

 *Coaching is partnering with clients in a thought-provoking and creative process that inspires them to maximize their personal and professional potential.—ICF*

The profession of coaching became increasingly widespread after this date. Professional Coach Thomas Leonard started the International Coaching Federation (ICF) in 1995 as a nonprofit organization for fellow coaches to support each other and grow the profession. The following year, a president was appointed and a board of directors established.

The organization, which outlines the ethical rules of coaching, provides accreditation for coaching programs and sets coaching standards, is active in more than 147 countries and boasts approximately 41,000 members. Today, coaching is defined as the process whereby individuals identify the goals they want to achieve in their personal or professional life and obtain support to make these goals a reality.

What Coaching Is and What It Is Not

A concise definition of coaching is a planned improvement relationship between a coach and a coachee. The purpose is for the person being coached to utilize the coach's support to obtain the goal they have set and learn how to overcome problems on their own. Every person and organization has a unique structure. Therefore, the solution in the coaching relationship is also within the individual or organization.

Coaching is a cooperative effort that effectively aids individuals and organizations improve themselves, enhance communication, solve problems, create, recognize opportunities, and experience success.

What Coaching Is

- A vehicle for learning and self-improvement.
- Supporting people toward their goals.
- Reciprocal sharing of experience and ideas for the purpose of achieving goals that have been set together.

What Coaching Is Not

- An opportunity to correct any person's behavior and actions.
- Directing any person to take measures that will ensure the goals are achieved.
- Being an expert or manager that knows all the answers.

Coaching in the Corporate Sphere

Managers must play many different roles in their work. One of those is the role of a coach. Whereas the manager mostly lays out the goal and strategy, the leader as a coach focuses on four things that we'll cover in the following chapters.

He must think of both his own interior thoughts, emotions, and worldview as well as of those of his team members while measuring the performance and behaviors of said individuals. Additionally, the team's shared ideas, values, and beliefs along with their collective performance, outcome, and the rules and procedures which they must abide by.

Comparing it to sports, if we look at Phil Jackson during his days as the coach of the Bulls, not only was he working individually with each member to bring out the best in them, but he had also built a cohesive team of players who otherwise weren't seen as GOATs (greatest of all time) outside of Jordan. On top of that, he also had to manage how certain players, such as Rodman due to his wildness and Jordan due to his ego, were seen by the world while he was suffering from outside pressure for the players he had chosen.

Coaching is a process that supports leadership development by providing an environment where people can talk about and debate themselves, share incidents related to the organization, and draw valuable conclusions from these discussions.

Executive Coaching is a managerial act that empowers individuals and teams and helps them achieve specific outcomes, discover their potential, and understand the moment and suitable conditions. The basic goal is to help executives and leaders discover themselves and develop their self-management abilities while facilitating their efforts to convert their potential into capacity.

With the aid of an Executive Coach, coachees will gain new insight about behaviors they were not aware of, which are hindering their development, and areas that will improve their performance. This one-on-one Corporate Coaching enhances an individual's competencies so that they experience a higher quality career and are capable of constructive change. This process helps coachees to examine themselves, engage in self-criticism, acquire different cognitive models, recognize opportunities, be more flexible, and engage in constructive change and development.

Executive Coaching is also focused on balancing career and personal life. We can define the competency capable of fulfilling the requirements of a professional career in parallel with a process of personal development supported by lifelong learning and awareness under the umbrella term of "leadership" as stages of awareness development and implementation.

Individuals with a certain level of knowledge and awareness—in other words, "those who know what needs to be done"—generally have difficulty answering the "how" question.

Leaders who have largely internalized their knowledge by living, learning, and self-development and have put it into practice with an original approach are the ones who rise to leadership positions in their circle of influence.

Group Coaching is a process of discovering and coming to grips with behaviors that the people in the group were previously unaware of and could not achieve on their own, behaviors that either lead to personal development or hinder it. This process is also a transformational experience that regulates interpersonal communication even as it facilitates awareness, positive change, and development. Reciprocal interaction helps calibrate the behavioral patterns that people are unaware of, but which are causing a breakdown in interpersonal relationships and leading to misunderstandings.

In Group Coaching, we create an environment where a person can see that the things they are afraid to say, the behaviors they hide and that they view as terrible weaknesses are actually things everyone struggles with. This brings much-needed relief, and their walls come down. What's more, being able to express oneself makes life itself easier. In short, it is a process that aims to help the people in the group quickly adapt to each other, to behave properly and to communicate well by ensuring that they understand themselves better.

Team Coaching

There are essentially two kinds of leadership: the old leadership style and contemporary leadership. The old leadership style was based on managing people, but the new leadership style is based on empowering people to be their best version of themselves. The essence of the new leadership style is management without micromanaging. Today, coaching is the most important competitive advantage and is a must in any organization. Every person has blind spots. The same is true of every organization. The secret power of coaching lies in converting these blind spots into perspective. What is expected of the new leader is not assessment but improvement and transitioning from being an expert to being a resource, from explaining things to asking good questions and adding the skills of a coach to his skill set.

 *Coming together is a start, staying together is progress, working together is success.*—Anonymous

In order to clearly see the whole, every individual needs to look at events with the perspective of an outsider. This is the answer to the question of why everyone needs coaching and feedback/feedforward. (Feedback focuses on the past, while feedforward focuses on the future.) Coaching helps teams understand and overcome the obstacles they face and move on to the next level of development. Coaching gives both the coach and the team brand-new perspectives.

Problems are not technical bottlenecks but motivational and relational.

Team Coaching is the process of helping people become a functioning team by uniting individuals in different functions and/or departments and helping them optimize their goal-oriented approach and actions. It is a process that helps the team formulate its agenda, objectives, and plans. The problems experienced in organizations are generally not technical but motivational and relational bottlenecks. With Team Coaching, these problems are addressed through active participation and awareness and solved by the members of the team. Team Coaching provides the support and guidance teams need to leverage their potential and move forward. The principle upon which Team Coaching is based is that the team and its members have the potential to achieve their objectives. In this case, the Team Coach is supporting the group's work as an interpreter/facilitator and guide. In all of these situations, the coach offers a path to constructive progress on the road to success.

The Team Coach may begin by identifying a unique mission, planning a project, and selecting team members, but the real work only begins after all of this is completed. The fact that people have come together does not immediately make them a team. They need support for this to happen. The job of the Team Coach is to transform these individuals into an integrated team devoted to a common mission. Every team has different characteristics, and they are all unique. A team is a living, dynamic system. Every incident, every act, every word impacts the team. A team has its own peculiar personality, unique psychological makeup, and vision. A team is a culture of verbal and nonverbal rules and values.

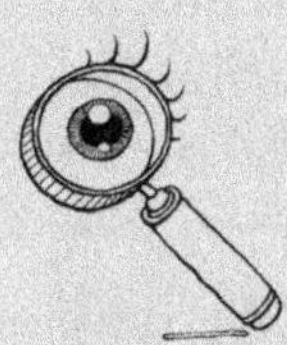

Hint

Important Factors in the Success of Team Coaching

A recent study asked managers what characteristics were required of an effective internal coach, and the following key factors were identified:

Being An Example And Having A Vision
They practice what they preach and instill it in the team.

Trustworthiness
They have won the team's confidence and foster support among team members.

Mutual Respect
They respect the team and are respected by the team.

Contact
They have effective communication skills.

Experience/Added Value
They have enough relevant experience to bring added value to the table.

Praise
They give positive feedback and feedforward.

The goal of Team Coaching is to make sure team members feel valued as a part of the team, to increase their contribution to the team, to help them appreciate the contribution of the other members and motivate each of them in the natural course of events. This work ensures that teams in an organization develop in tandem, work together better, and achieve productive outcomes. Unlike other approaches to coaching, the objectives and success of the team are paramount.

The Benefits of Team Coaching for the Team and the Organization

- It increases productivity by ensuring that team members understand each other and their needs.
- It brings fun to the workplace to raise spirits and boost excitement, enthusiasm, and creativity.
- It creates loyalty to the organization by increasing job satisfaction and reducing costs.
- Employees with a higher level of personal satisfaction create a better experience for both internal and external customers, which boosts customer satisfaction.
- It ensures the continued vitality of the organization by fostering a dynamic and stable environment.
- It gives team members new perspectives, new possibilities, and new opportunities for learning.
- It is the most human-focused approach to performance management.
- It ensures that teams are sustainable and consistently successful.
- It creates a social process focused on trust and achievement.
- It helps people discover what it means to be a team.
- It reduces or eliminates costs, strengthening the team and the individuals by creating joint outcomes.
- It achieves effective results.

The Difference Coaching Makes

Coaching works as a facilitator of communication so that events can be viewed from a broader perspective. When team members speak, the coach helps other members listen like a Team Coach. The coach knows how to listen to the comments from members. The Team Coach realizes that in all communication the "other side" could be right, and that the ability to see the objective from a broader perspective may be found beyond the current options.

The Team Coach should be trying to understand what the team is trying to say. Fully aware that the options are not always black and white, the Team Coach helps members hear the voices that oppose the ideas they believe in. It is important that team members share their perspective on events and see the differences between their perspective and that of others. The Team Coach should encourage the team to think out loud, especially on topics that are difficult to express.

Integral Approach with Teams

Since the early 1900s, the advances in many fields, particularly industry, and mankind's drive for perfection and progress have encouraged individuals to seek new ways, methods, and approaches to realizing their full potential.

Ken Wilber, a philosopher, thinker, and practitioner who studies approaches and systems both in history and today, built the most comprehensive approach yet developed with the Integral Model, the foundation of which was laid in the 1990s. The Integral Model is an unerring map based on five basic elements: Quadrants, Lines, Levels, States, and Types.

Quadrants are the foundation of the model and are based on the individual, the perceptions and observations created by the individual in their sphere, the organizations that they interact with, and the system they live in.

The journey undertaken by the Team Coach and the team begins with their internalization of these four different perspectives and continues as a constantly self-renewing dynamic process that ranges from ideas to assessment.

"Me" (Intention), "It" (Behavior), "We" (Culture), and "Its" (System). In other words, the four quadrants, the four basic perspectives in any situation, the ways of looking at anything, become quite simple.

	INTERNAL	EXTERNAL
INDIVIDUAL	INTENTIONAL	BEHAVIORAL
COLLECTIVE	CULTURAL	SYSTEMIC

Which of these perspectives is correct? According to the integral approach, all of them are. They are what an event looks like to you from different perspectives. If you deny or ignore any of these perspectives, that is when the problems start to appear. The four quadrants must be present within the integral perspective.

Quadrants are what the internal and external parts of the individual and society are. The issue here is that when we want to have an integrated perspective, all four quadrants must be simultaneously involved.

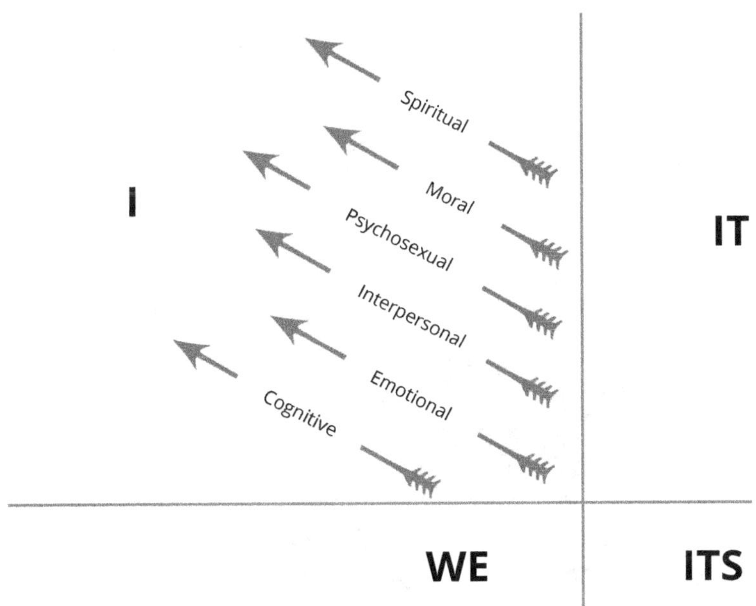

All four quadrants exhibit growth, development, and evolution. In other words, all of them have their own levels and stages of development. However, these stages are not sharply defined, like the steps of a ladder. They manifest themselves as fluid waves of development. This occurs throughout the natural world. The oak tree emerges from an acorn and grows through various stages of development.

How Is the Integral Approach Used on Integrated Teams?

The integral approach requires that individuals look at life through different lenses so that their understanding of the situations they find themselves in is made clearer and more productive with different perspectives, which then inform their decisions and activities. The goal here is for all of the team members to be aware of the different perspectives and effectively implement them in their life. Team members that have this awareness will generate more effective outcomes working together, and the results will be much more sustainable.

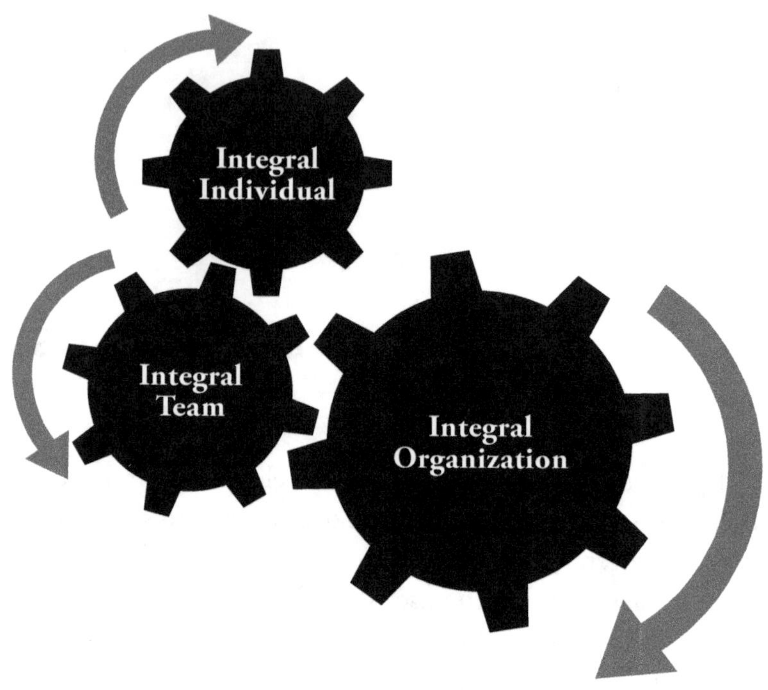

Awareness + Understanding + Action = Results

The team will see an important difference when they achieve personal integration. The entire organization will be affected in a positive and active manner with the birth of an active integrated team that achieves its goals, which in turn will begin to make a difference in the entire system. Another of the primary goals is for all of the individuals in an organization to trust each other and communicate effectively with one another.

Individuals on integrated teams are able to identify problems, situations and events due to their awareness and unique perspectives. They will then consider the necessary strategies, recommend solutions and alternatives, and implement them. In this way, they develop the ability to effectively reach goals and keep this skill sharp.

Setting the right goals and contributing to a common purpose is just as important for the team as achieving goals. This is an area that must be considered as a whole as well.

Integrated Individual

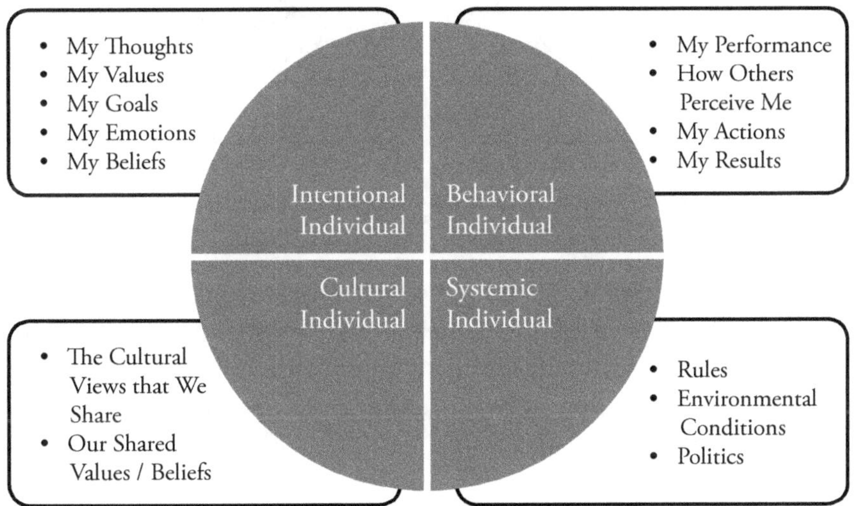

Goal: Integrated Individuals

- They are aware of their potential and realize it.
- Individuals realize how they are integrated.
- They identify their needs.
- They identify their reason for existing.
- They realize the value they bring to the team.
- They become aware of their personal goals.
- They clarify the meaning of the event/purpose/process/goal/ result variable for themselves and for the team.

Integrated Team

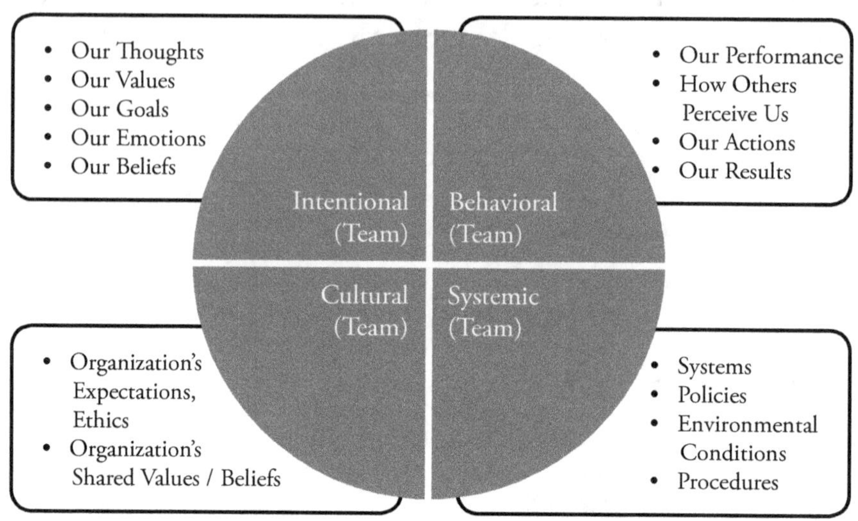

Goal: Integrated Team

- Creates the prerequisites for being a team: trust, managing conflict, adherence to joint decisions, being open to accountability, paying attention to results.
- The team understands and defines itself as a system.
- The team identifies its own needs.
- It clarifies its goals.
- It understands other individuals and creates an understanding of what it means to be "Us."
- It develops mutual intelligences and emotions.
- The team effectively achieves learning and development in a shorter period of time with the coach's support.
- The team takes responsibility for the attitudes, behaviors, and approaches it exhibits.
- It recognizes the relationships between individual goals and team goals.
- It implements what it learns from its experience in different areas.
- The result is a tough team and individuals that support and empower one another as they overcome obstacles.

- The team recognizes developments, resistance, and conflict on the road to achieving its goals, and the result is transformation.
- It is possible to observe and manage the team's stages of development.
- Action plans are created to reach goals.

Goal: Integrated Organization

- When teams trust each other and work faithfully toward a common goal, it changes the nature of the entire organization.
- Teams take more specific steps toward the organization's vision, values, and objectives.
- The performance of teams that speak the same language and share the same values quickly bolsters motivation in the organization.
- They unveil the hidden potential of the organization and sharpen its competitive edge.

Model of Integrated Team Coaching

Our goal in *Better Leaders, Better Teams* is to ensure that the executives in the organization move from managing to creating a portrait of the future, which is vital for each team member, the team, and the organization to achieve, and to effectively support and develop the system as it works toward this goal.

Our goal is to ensure that the executives in the organization move from managing and coaching individuals to

- managing teams,
- empowering teams,
- converting potential to capacity and working as a Team Coach. And to support the creation of the Team Coach's toolbox while they are doing all these things, to increase awareness and to help overcome obstacles that pop up while trying to reach goals.

2 FIRST STEPS IN TEAM COACHING

The First Step Is Knowing Yourself

 *I can only discover Me in You.*—Sami Bugay

It was a difficult time. The dollar was rising like a hot-air balloon while our company was trying to reduce its costs, and we told our department managers to quickly rank the most effective employees with the best performance from good to fair. I will never forget the objection raised by one team leader, who said, "Mr. Bugay, how can I know which of my colleagues will perform better in the future? I don't think I can make that decision by looking at their attitudes up until now. Besides, I now realize that I have not observed them that closely anyway. This is going to be exceedingly difficult." I asked myself that same question back then. What would I do if faced with the same situation? It is only now that I can see how in my previous experience as a manager, my lack of knowledge about both myself and my teammates threatened our common future.

As a team coach, the first step that we must take toward common goals is to foster the trust created as everyone, starting with the leaders, understands themselves and gets to know the members of the team.

 *Wisdom is recognizing truth. Wisdom is knowing yourself. If you do not know yourself, all your studies are in vain.* —Yunus Emre

First Steps in Team Coaching: Getting to Know Each Other

Beginning with activities that break the ice in a team environment not only helps everyone relax, but it also raises the level of sincerity. The first interaction between team members should take place in a warm and friendly environment. There is a need to be sensitive to the levels of engagement and commitment until everyone feels safe. Resistance is an obstacle to the learning process. These types of activities help the team members shift the focus from themselves to the team so they can see the big picture. Furthermore, because participation is required, everyone has a chance to be heard. These activities take the form of short questions, funny stories, or games, and are further enriched by the use of metaphor.

ACTIVITY

Getting to Know Each Other

Purpose: Break the ice, develop openness, and experience the power of using metaphors in coaching.

Duration: 20 minutes.

Materials: Notepad and pen.
"Allow me to introduce you to ..."
In this paired exercise, the first thing that the participants do is choose a partner. One will be person A and the other person B. For example, during the exercise, the person with the longest hair can be A and the person with the shortest hair can be B. Person A asks questions first. The exercise lasts a total of 20 minutes, with ten minutes given to A and ten minutes to B.
A: Allow me to introduce you to B!
A asks B questions to learn about the following issues.

Things they love about their job and think are important:

____

____

____

___________ ____________________________________

Other things they love and think are important:

____

____

____

____

Things that you don't know about them and which will surprise you:

____

____

____

____

A will try to describe B by comparing them to a food. A will consider the following situation.

A: This food tastes like_______________________________

Then A and B will switch places.

After each participant shares, the Team Coach will ask the entire group what they discovered about themselves. This new awareness will be shared with the team.

The Use of Metaphor in Team Coaching

A metaphor is the use of a concept in a novel way by means of comparison. It is also known as a figure of speech. Metaphors are employed artistically to make communication more effective and spice up the language. They add beauty, power, vibrancy, elegance, depth, and scope to the narrative. They help illustrate emotions with words.

 *As Kandilli swam in slumber, we dragged the moonshine across the waters.*—Yahya Kemal Beyatlı

Metaphor is a technique used to teach new ideas. It is an enormously powerful learning and teaching tool that has been shown to help people remember the information that they learn.

In coaching, metaphor is used to illustrate a point and to paint a verbal picture for the coachee. It provides the coachee with clues about perspective on life. Metaphors help people develop their creativity, provide a tangible angle on concepts that are difficult to express, and make it easy to remember new information.

 *The thorns that prick your feet herald the approach of the Rose you seek.*—Mevlâna Celâleddin-i Rûmî

The metaphors that you use affect your thoughts, feelings, and actions. The metaphors used to represent a relationship change the emotions and attitudes in the relationship. Look at the metaphors you use to express your feelings about a topic you have negative feelings about. Realize that the metaphor you use to escape this particular mood is directing your feelings. Your mood changes the moment you represent something differently in your mind. Every metaphor you adopt brings with it a series of principles, ideas, and prejudices.

Interaction Between Team Members

According to the integrated perspective, the whole consists of its parts, but the parts do not individually represent the whole. On the contrary, these parts are defined by the characteristics of the whole. When viewed in this way, individuals are part of their environment, and we cannot even see the individual apart from the environment.

Each individual not only reacts to their environment, but they also affect it. They are both a cause and a result of what they experience in their contact with their environment.

In order to assess and improve how we define ourselves strategically, we need to look at our relationships with other individuals. When we understand how we affect others and what we trigger in them, we can gain greater insights into ourselves. When it comes to obtaining honest "feedback," which is the key to improvement, it is essential to build trust. This also requires a desire to boost confidence and courage.

The cultural discourse of an organization is shaped by the values and norms of a society, like nested systems. If an organization has many offices in different regions of the world, this changes the culture of the organization and especially virtual teams.

Making a Contract

Ahmet entered the room exasperated. "That's it. I can't take this anymore." He was an entrepreneur in his early forties with years of experience as an executive, a man who had started his own company and overcome countless difficulties. This was the fourth meeting we had had since I started working with him as a coach.

I won't lie. I was used to being greeted at the door to start our meeting, but that didn't happen. I was curious and immediately asked, "I hope everything is okay, Ahmet. I'm not used to seeing you like this. I am curious. Is it something you want to talk about?" "Well, Sami, it is just really starting to irritate the heck out of me. How many times has this happened? You know that we are a four-person management team, but in spite of the fact that we are all mature, serious people, whenever we have a difference of opinion, the gentleman façade comes crashing down and we start acting like teenagers. This not only has a negative impact on us as individuals but on the whole company. It is demoralizing. We are wasting our energy arguing over problems instead of using it to boost morale and come up with solutions. After the aggression and adrenaline subside, we talk about how we can move toward common goals in this business and create an atmosphere where we can hold each other accountable if necessary. There is no problem as long as the atmosphere is calm, but God forbid anyone should have a different opinion."

Although we may not be aware of it, making contracts is a crucial dynamic in our lives. From the school we attend, our friendships, and our colleagues, to the company we choose to work at, marriage, divorce, and every opportunity where we choose to share, we are dealing with a contract. How are we choosing to work as a team? What kind of atmosphere and shared goals do we want to create? If we do not have the same opinions and ideas on the road we travel, how are we going to travel it together? What are some behavioral or pragmatic approaches?

Reaching an agreement as a team and actually signing a physical contract, and even hanging this up in the team members' shared space as a visual reminder is an effective way to maintain our focus.

First Steps in Team Coaching: Making a Team Agreement

A team agreement includes clearly specified objectives as well as the goals and actions that have been agreed upon. It determines the team's vision, mission, values, and operating principles.

As a Team Coach, we can begin our work by laying down specific rules that define a modus operandi and ensure harmony. Defining the basic rules of the team with team consensus will help the team concentrate on using its time and energy effectively.

A team agreement helps the team members take responsibility for how they work. Taking responsibility is like the central nervous system of every professional relationship. In a business environment where people take personal responsibility, individuals can embrace their work and say, "The ball is in my court." This reduces the tendency for individuals to blame each other and ask others to do their work.

As a Team Coach, it is important to help the team set and proudly implement their own rules. The team will need help structuring their team agreement. The one thing that must be remembered is that the Team Coach is also part of the team. A team agreement is a dynamic agreement. Articles can be added, and some articles can be amended based on need and changing circumstances.

We Are Number One!

Purpose: Creating a strong team identity.

Duration: 20 minutes.

Materials: Presentation paper, markers, tape, scissors, and various handicraft materials.

The team will create its own group identity. For example, they will choose a mascot and create a logo like a football team.

The participants are divided into groups of five. The first step is to brainstorm. The goal is to find creative ideas with input from everyone.

Each group is given four minutes. They are asked to brainstorm who they are and what they are about. The following questions are written on the presentation paper to kick off the discussion:

- How would you describe your team?
- What does this team do?
- As individuals, who does the team consist of?
- To what could you compare the team?
- What is something fantastic about the team?

After the brainstorming is completed, all of the teams meet together and are asked to discuss who they are and what they are about.

One person volunteers to write down the basic ideas on the presentation paper. Now all of the team's ideas have been collected on a single piece of paper.

In the next step, different tasks are given to the same five-person groups.

- Select a team name.
- Make a team logo.
- Create a team mascot.
- Write a team slogan.

After all the groups have completed these tasks, each group will be asked to present their ideas, after which they will consider and discuss the following questions:

- What are the benefits of having a team identity?
- What are creative ways to strengthen your identity in your daily work routine?

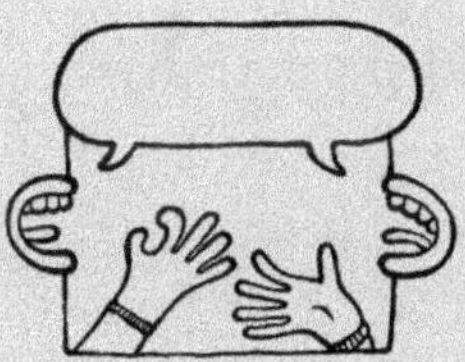

Discussion Time

During group work, the characteristics of great teams and terrible teams are shared with the whole group.

Team Agreement

Write the principles that you have decided to implement as a team in the empty fields below.

If you were living and working together on a new planet, what kind of planet would you want it to be? What should the climate and atmosphere be?

____

____

____

Which behaviors should be permitted among the people living on this planet?

____

____

____

What kind of communication methods would you prefer on this planet and how would each be used?

____

____

____

When something goes wrong on this planet, what approach should be used to set things right? Who would take responsibility, and what would that look like?

____

____

____

What methods/conditions would be specified for the use of common resources on the planet?

____

____

____

What are the five most fundamental values that would be implemented on this planet?

____

____

____

Individual Commitment to the Team

____

____

____

Atmosphere

What kind of atmosphere do you want to create among your-selves today?

____

____

____

Which of your behaviors will foster/ensure this atmosphere?

____

____

____

Which of your behaviors will be an obstacle to this atmosphere?

____

____

How do you want to treat each other in difficult situations (differences of opinion, strained relationships)?

____

____

____

Team Agreement

Essential Features Of My Own Team Agreement

In the space below, work with your group to list the issues (goals, methodology, action, obstacles, etc.) that your team must agree on and discuss them. Share why it is important for you that these issues be addressed and discussed on the team. (Use additional paper if necessary.)

Discussion Time

In what areas of life are you able to implement the idea of making agreements? Discuss the dynamic nature of these agreements and being able to make changes based on need.

The Importance of the Team Atmosphere

In his book *Social Intelligence*, Daniel Goleman describes how trauma and emotional instability prevent the brain's execution center from operating properly. People cannot concentrate on anything or think clearly when their emotions are frayed.

In terms of the brain, the biology of anxiety moves us away from excellence and compromises the brain's cognitive efficiency. The reason is that fear traumatizes the mind and derails creativity and learning.

When the mind is operating in a state of internal harmony, its efficiency, speed, and power are maximized. Neuroscientist Antonio Damasio calls it the state of greatest harmony.

An inverted U curve demonstrates the relationship between cognitive performance, like learning or decision-making, and stress levels. Stress is proportional to strain.

While a low level of difficulty leads to boredom, as the level of difficulty increases, so do anxiety and unhappiness. When the level of difficulty becomes insurmountable, stress intensifies while our ability to perform and learn collapses.

Within normal limits, pressure boosts motivation and facilitates concentration. However, stress beyond an optimal level has a negative effect on cognitive efficiency.

These effects can be seen in leaders as well. Negative emotions reduce empathy and attention. Negative team leaders only focus on the negative characteristics of their subordinates, so their performance evaluations are more negative, and they draw conclusions that are more negative than warranted.

There is no doubt that our psychological state has a direct effect on performance. That is why leaders have a single unchanging emotional responsibility: To help people get as close as they can to the top of the inverted U curve and stay there.

A leader must never forget that emotions are contagious. A small scolding skillfully applied can boost a team's attentiveness and motivation. Many effective leaders intuitively understand that a display of frustration in just the right dose boosts energy levels.

Remember that people in any group pay more attention to the words and actions of the most influential person present. The transfer of psychological state from a leader to their followers is observed in every relationship where one person has power over another. This is why the emotions of leaders are contagious. In spite of the power difference in the relationships, they all have a good and hidden power because they hold the key to the development and improvement of the weaker person. The members of a group all contribute their own flavor to create a diverse emotional soup. However, the strongest spice is that contributed by the leader, because everyone is watching this person.

In order to measure the power that emotions have on people, fifty-six leaders were put into either a good or bad mood, and the emotional effect this had on the groups they managed was measured. Individuals on the teams led by positive leaders reported feeling better about themselves. Even more importantly, they completed more work with less effort. The harmony on the teams with negative leaders was compromised, and they were less efficient.

What's worse, the frenetic energy expended to satisfy the demanding leaders resulted in them making poor decisions and adopting the wrong strategies.

When leaders take a negative approach to motivate their employees, they may think that the team gets more work done. But this does not always mean it is better-quality work. Constant negativity disrupts the group's energy and hurts morale.

In a sense, leadership is a series of social interactions. Subordinates can sense the leader's empathy, support, attentiveness, and positive attitude in healthy interactions. In unhealthy interactions, the person/team feels like they are an abstract number and like they are threatened.

People more clearly remember the negative interactions with their superiors and in more detail than they do the positive interactions. When a leader is insensitive, they not only increase the risk of losing good personnel, they also reduce cognitive efficiency.

A leader with a high level of social intelligence helps the team manage its emotional difficulties and pull itself together.

In view of the fact that emotions are highly contagious, team leaders do well to remember that they have the power to make the situation better or worse.

Emotions between colleagues can have a huge impact on the effectiveness of both, and a leader may be the only one to clear the air or correct conflict between colleagues through his power to change the dynamic.

First Steps in Team Coaching:
Understanding the Members of the Team

The extent to which we feel "happy" in our lives as individuals depends largely on our ability to establish good relationships with ourselves and with other people. The friction between team members, employees, friends, spouses, or politicians is caused by the fact that the dynamics which determine individual behavior are different. When we understand our own behavior profile, it is easier to explain who we are and why we do what we do. In the same way, we gain a deeper understanding of the behavior of others.

As a Team Coach, knowing the behavioral dynamics of your team members and making sure that the team members also understand these dynamics will give you important advantages when observing and coaching the team. This awareness is an issue that must be handled delicately both in terms of team members and the Team Coach at more advanced levels.

When the team members figure out each other's behavioral dynamics, they will have accepted the points of view arising from different perspectives. Looking at things from different perspectives will enrich the team.

All of us have a system or process that we use to determine what any event in our lives means for us and how we need to respond. Everyone has a different take on what happens depending on their perspective. The first thing that affects all of our assessments is our mental and emotional state when we make the assessment.

 *Man is an eye, a viewpoint. Everything else is flesh. Man is only as valuable as what his eyes see.*
—Mevlâna Celâleddin-i Rûmî

Our objective is to take advantage of everything in our lives in a way that will always give us the results that we want. We can take the rudder and manage what we do with the events in our lives. If we make conscious decisions about the emotional atmosphere we want to create and look at things from a perspective that will ensure this atmosphere, we can take responsibility for ourselves, our team, and the entire organization.

Examples of Different Perspectives:

When I change my perspective, I make it possible to find different solutions to events and issues.

In this regard, one of the primary functions of a team coach is to change the perspectives that team members have to a fresh approach that is different from the daily and familiar routine and that encourages and guides them to move out of their comfort zones.

Elements in Nature and Behavioral Dynamics

According to the philosophies of antiquity, everything we see is a combination of fire, earth, air, and water. The philosophies of the Middle East and the Far East made these elements the foundation, and they based their philosophies about everything from health to architecture on these elements. Carl Gustav Jung used these four elements as a foundation for grouping types of people, making four main categories of human characteristics: feeling (fire), the five senses (earth), reason (air), and intuition (water).

This approach has been used for many years in various studies on leadership, teams, and groups that examine humans (which are a part of nature) and their behavior.

The most famous Japanese samurai, the undefeated samurai Miyamoto Musashi, born in 1584, wrote a masterpiece entitled *The Book of Five Rings* about the Musashi art of war. He uses the four elements of earth, water, fire and air as a basis for leadership development and strategies of war and says that the void is the foundation that makes all of them possible.

The Book of Five Rings is the fundamental resource of all martial arts, but the undergirding philosophy, which is influenced by Zen, Shinto and Confucian thought, is also applied to many areas of modern life outside of philosophy and the martial arts. It is a strategy book that is frequently referenced in the world of business today. For example, many Japanese businessmen organize their sales campaigns like a military campaign with the same energy that motivated Musashi.

Elements and Our Worldview

Each of the four elements of fire, air, earth, or water represents a fundamental energy and type of consciousness. These elements help us understand a person's perception of the world as well as the instincts and reactions that make them do what they do. It gives us insight into how a person acts.

Fire symbolizes courage and willpower, earth represents patience and discipline, air is related to perception, comprehension, and making associations, while water is the representation of nurture and feeling.

The Element of Fire

In Japanese, *ka* or *hi* means fire and reflects the energy or powerful forces that move the world. Fire is movement, action, initiation, and leadership. It is the element of adventure. It is joyous and exuberant. It generates heat and light. It is the element of passion, attraction, creativity, chance, and power. Fire is associated with high motivation and enthusiasm. The element of fire is always courageous and teaches one how to survive no matter what life throws at them.

Musashi describes the time to fight in the fire strategies. During battle, a samurai must quickly respond to the changing moves of his opponent. He must be able to adjust his own rhythm, make snap decisions, and quickly change his strategy. In order to accomplish this, he must make practice part of his daily routine. Whether the fire is big or small, or whether one is facing a single opponent or many does not matter. The spirit of battle is the same. As long as the samurai maintains the same courageous spirit, he can overcome any fire.

The Element of Earth

In Japanese, *chi* or *tsuchi* means earth or soil and represents the solid substances of the world. We see the simplest expression of earth in rocks, which do not easily react to change, but are held tightly and embraced by the soil. Earth represents the five senses and the body. It is the foundation of material existence. Durability, determination, patience, and disciplined toil are associated with the earth. The earth also encompasses fertility, protection, and compassion.

When he describes his war strategies, Musashi begins with earth. The first thing that a swordsman needs to do when preparing for battle is formulate a detailed strategy. He must consider every tiny detail like a map written in the earth. The first secret to winning is to begin with a detailed strategy and work on it diligently.

The Element of Water

In Japanese, water is called *sui* or *mizu*, and it represents the fluid substances of the world. Water is the element associated with the emotions, love, and the sentimental body. It adapts and accepts change easily. Water has also become the symbol of instincts. Water heals and nourishes. It channels our sincerity, support, memory, and change. It is viewed as a symbol of wisdom because of its ability to reflect reality. It is mysterious and intrinsic. Water teaches us how to join the flow.

Water is the second book in the *Five Rings*. Just as water can take any shape, a warrior must internalize the strategy he employs, make it a part of his spirit, and feel it in his body. Results cannot be achieved from strategies that are developed through memorization, reading, or imitation. Every samurai must develop his own strategy and live this out in his spirit and body. The body must be master of all knowledge. It must determine its own actions, be still when necessary, but a raging torrent when required.

The Element of Air

In Japanese, air is *fu* or *kaze,* and it represents growth, development, and freedom of movement. Air is associated with the mind that is capable of making decisions. Concise ideas are expressed with a high level of awareness. Air symbolizes intelligence, communication, and knowledge. It rules the world of words, contracts, science, technology, hope, and communication. Another positive aspect of air is optimism, which is associated with guiding the mind. Being optimistic is the ability to focus on what is good in even the toughest moments. Analytical thinking, categorization, and planning are also connected with the air.

The air book of the *Five Rings* emphasizes the importance of knowing everything related to your rivals. It is impossible for a samurai to know others before he knows himself. Every strategy is based on a different foundation. It is important to recognize and understand different methods, both those used in the past and those used today. The samurai cannot fully internalize the foundations of his own strategy until he gathers knowledge and understands others.

The last theme in the *Five Rings* is "void." The samurai must use the harmony and rhythm in nature as his example and be in harmony with it himself as well. This is the only way he can fight his enemy naturally.

These four elements are found in different measures in every individual. They influence each other and define individual characteristics. The kaleidoscope of human personality types reflects the infinite diversity of the relationship between these elements. No one consists of just a single element. Any view from a single window cannot describe our worldview. Everyone is a composite of these elements in different measures.

Imbalance between the elements can affect individuals in different ways.

ELEMENT	If Excessive
FIRE	<ul><li>These people are overly self-confident.</li><li>May be overly ambitious.</li><li>May seem selfish.</li><li>Have a tendency to be extreme.</li><li>Take risks without weighing the consequences.</li><li>Have difficulty noticing problems because they are so focused on the goal.</li><li>Easily irritated.</li><li>May exhibit aggressive behavior.</li><li>Can be hurtful to those in their circle.</li><li>Hyperactive.</li><li>May be restless.</li><li>Appear to be extremely busy.</li><li>May have trouble in personal relationships.</li><li>May be insensitive.</li><li>Appear impetuous.</li><li>Tend to be bossy.</li></ul>

	If Deficient
	<ul><li>May lack courage and feel insecure.</li><li>May be slow in taking action.</li><li>May take time to overcome significant problems in their life.</li><li>Indecisive.</li><li>Unable to express themselves strongly.</li><li>Lack motivation.</li><li>Avoid conflict.</li><li>Are low on energy and enthusiasm.</li><li>Are not extremely ambitious and don't have strong willpower.</li><li>Lack enthusiasm for life.</li><li>May have low self-esteem and be afraid to express themselves.</li><li>Tend to suppress their anger.</li></ul>

ELEMENT	If Excessive
EARTH	• Excessive interest in the physical world manifests itself in lack of idealism or imagination, and narrow-mindedness. • Their dependence on extreme orderliness and routine can be detrimental to the individual in the long term. • Not open to change. • Inflexible and have strict rules. • Cannot pursue vision and have limited creativity due to their constant pursuit of tangible things. • Excessive perfectionism can lead to a constantly critical perspective. • Do not take time to relax and have fun. • Can be overly critical of themselves. • Social relationships can be affected because they cannot appreciate others. • Their vision can be narrow because they accept everything as it is. • Their dependence on operational systems can prevent them from action to improve the system. • Do not take risks. • Are skeptical. • Their lives are dominated by work and practical matters. If these are threatened, their self-confidence suffers. • Excessive fondness for material things can create ethical problems. • They can appear narrow-minded and dependent on order and routine.

ELEMENT	If Deficient
EARTH	• They are unable to live in harmony with the physical world. • Ignore the necessities of worldly life, but when they begin to face financial difficulty, they may gain understanding in this area. • May have a feeling of not belonging to this world. • May fail to implement their ideas. • Everything may feel like a challenge due to lack of practicality. • Overly conservative and not open to new ideas. • Must learn to accept making mistakes and sometimes go with the flow. • May have a need for security because they feel rootless and detached. • May neglect physical and worldly needs.

ELEMENT	If Excessive
	• Fragile, sulky, easily offended, anxious, overly subjective, and seldom rational. • Neglect themselves because they think of others too much. • Live in a fantasy world with their head in the clouds. • Mysterious and deep thinkers. • Having too much of the water element can be compared to being on the ocean without sail or rudder, blown every which way by the wind. • May experience a loss of identity due to excessive sacrifice and devotion. • Expect others to fill their inner void. • Profound longing is triggered by desires and insecurities. • Overly sensitive. • May overreact to the smallest provocation. • May be constantly anxious and feel the need to protect themselves. • As they are full of emotion, they feel the need to actively utilize their emotions by taking an interest in other people due to their sensitivity and empathy. • May display obsessive behavior. • Have a tendency to be extreme in their actions.

WATER	If Deficient
	• These people are characterized by lack of emotion, inability to express emotions or feel empathy. • Lack self-confidence. • Unable to utilize intuition and may be cruel. • Underdeveloped imagination. • Have difficulty understanding and sharing their emotions. • Unaware of emotional needs. • Are harsh and lacking in compassion. • May be cold and distant. • Do not trust intuitive knowledge. • Are very afraid of suffering and are unwilling to confront their own emotions. • Need emotional attachment.

ELEMENT	If Excessive
AIR	• They may have their head in the clouds, be detached from reality and have Utopian ideas. • Flamboyant and tend to exaggerate freedom. • Have difficulty setting boundaries in relationships. • Talk too much but don't know how to listen. • May be scornful and derisive. • May be overly extroverted and constantly generating ideas but unable to implement them. • Have an overly active mind that needs to be directed and controlled. • Live in their mind. • May be content with superficial information and not care about the details of the things they are interested in. • Cannot get organized; may be disorderly and without schedule. • Because their mind is hyperactive, they may experience an impaired nervous system. • They need to be appreciated and are motivated by approval. • Act quickly because they are not detailed. • May change their mind quickly. • Not very aware of intense emotions and physical limits. • Afraid that their opinions will not be valued.

ELEMENT	If Deficient
AIR	• May have difficulty forming relationships. • May have trouble with comprehension and perception. • May feel misunderstood and be unable to express themselves verbally. • Cannot be objective, and have trouble looking at events objectively. • Have difficulty embracing new ideas and different people. • May not have a neutral perspective and have trouble expressing themselves. • Unable to analyze situations and so do not benefit from reason. • It is difficult for them to view their own behaviors and undertakings from the outside. • Self-awareness is a struggle. • Have trouble developing social relationships.

The Use of Elements on Teams

When the team's element balance is viewed as a whole, the strengths born of the dominant elements are noticeable, and more effective solutions can be developed for the obstacles presented by the deficient elements. Proper matches can be made among team actors. The best job descriptions will be created based on personality characteristics. The right personnel will be hired for open positions. When people are assigned to jobs that match their characteristics, they are more motivated. As the differences in the fundamental values of the team members become clear, problems can be resolved without making them personal. People are more tolerant and the language of communication changes.

In her book *The Four Elements of Success,* Laurie Beth Jones talks about how personal elements affect the team based on detailed research that provides invaluable insight. The information in this chapter is based on Jones's work.

An earth team leader needs to learn how to do analysis, a water leader how to make decisions quickly, an air leader how to be patient when dealing with details. A fire leader, on the other hand, wants to be the center of attention and needs recognition.

It is important that a team leader ensure balance and understand the combination of elements on the team to obtain effective results. Too much water extinguishes fire. Too much air turns earth into dust in the wind. Too much fire can be caustic. If water and earth are not properly combined, the result can be mud. A team without air cannot breathe and is unable to change. Without earth, there is no balance and order. Everything will seem to be hanging in the air. When there is not enough water, we see problems with poor communication. Without fire, the strength and courage to start new ventures is lacking. The leader can obtain more effective results by granting more freedom and authority to predominantly fire members by being more supportive of water members and showing them appreciation, by giving earth members clear goals and adequate time, and by allowing air members to feel liberated.

The following table describes the shadow aspects of team members from each element, their characteristics, and relationships with one another.

Shadow Aspects of the Elements

ELEMENT	FIRE	EARTH	WATER	AIR
SHADOWS	Maverick	Boring	Slow	Disorganized
	Selfish	Stingy	Unstable	Careless
	Fearless	Harsh	Untrustworthy	Unfocused
	Judgmental	Hard-hearted	Quiet	Reactionary
	Dominant	Slow	Procrastinator	Demanding
	Ill-tempered	Hard-headed	Overly sensitive	Inconsistent
	Insensitive	Legalistic	Ineffective	Untrustworthy

The Use of Elements on Teams

What Kind of Team Member Is Fire?

- They are enthusiastic and passionate and illuminate their surroundings.
- Do not shrink back from an argument. Defend their ideas fiercely.
- Love excitement and action.
- Do not want to get stuck in the past. The future is always more important to them.
- Do not like routine and a slow pace.
- Are quick to take action. Take responsibility, make decisions, and implement them.
- Can focus on many different jobs at once.
- Are strong enough to easily complete challenging jobs. Expect others to do the same.
- Like adventure, and uncertainty is exciting for them.
- Want to set their own rules. Are motivated by achieving goals.
- Result-focused.
- Not detail oriented. Want to understand the essence of the matter.
- Speak directly without beating around the bush.
- Do not like losing control or being ordinary.
- Want to be seen as the leader in whatever setting they are in.
- Want to be free in the workplace. Routine work is boring for them.
- Are happy to have support as they do not want to mess with details.
- Want to work in a setting where they feel responsible.
- Capable of seeing the big picture and delegating tasks.
- Direct, challenging team member that speaks their mind.
- Prefer to teach instead of learning.
- Once they have enough information to reach their goal, the details do not interest them.
- Can work without tiring.
- Constantly generating exciting new ideas and goals.
- Love competition, and this is reflected in their relationships.
- Have a high tolerance for stress.
- Go-getter. Prefer to do things rather than talk about them.
- Need to be reminded of the existence of other team members when focused on a goal.

What Kind of Team Member Is Earth?

- They are not initiators but collect information and do research.
- Self-confident, trustworthy, and consistent.
- Prefer safety and planning over risk taking.
- Do not lose control and do not like displays of emotion.
- Respect authority and are comforted by rules and order.
- React slowly to change. Change is scary because they have a low tolerance for mistakes.
- Realistic and value ideas and reason.
- Avoid emotional settings and conflict.
- Make rational explanations because they have good command of details.
- Their biggest fear is making a mistake.
- Do not like to take risks.
- Establish their perfect comfort zone and do not want to leave it.
- Want to be rewarded for doing good work.
- Like to work in quiet settings alone or in small groups.
- Their work area is clean and neat.
- Like to plan and to have an excellent command of details.
- In crisis, they keep their cool and provide order.
- Love boundaries, and their roles and tasks must be defined with clear rules.
- Uncomfortable with emotionalism, lack of discipline, and lack of rules.
- Work comfortably when there are specified objectives and a set, orderly routine.
- Need to do a detailed analysis when making decisions.
- Setting up a system and being organized are important.
- Do not trust easily.
- Establish strong relationships that take time.
- Mutual respect is important.
- Uncertainty creates stress.
- Avoid reactionary behavior.
- Engage in self-criticism.
- Believe that success will come in the long term with determination and work.
- Desire clarity.
- Bring quality and efficiency to the projects they participate in.
- Need time to complete the work they are assigned.

What Kind of Team Member Is Water?

- They are relaxed and sincere, generate solutions, and bring balance and harmony to relationships.
- Understanding expectations and discernment regarding the environment is important. Do not act quickly.
- Do not like inconsistency or challenging situations.
- Patient with good control of emotions.
- Do not like authority and have their own way of doing things.
- Do not adapt quickly to change, so they need consistency and assurance.
- Good listeners.
- Comfortable in settings with warm, friendly relationships.
- Prefer to quietly observe rather than getting involved in every conversation.
- Are peacemakers in conflicts between people. For them, harmony is paramount.
- Conflict and differences of opinion are not pleasant for them.
- Love to be part of a team and succeed together.
- Can work in any setting as long as there is consistency and harmony. Do not like to be rushed.
- Bring sincerity and warmth wherever they go.
- Cooperation and joint decisions enable them to demonstrate their potential comfortably.
- Prefer traditional methods over new techniques when it comes to learning. Want to know the practical application of knowledge.
- May have difficulty setting priorities. Do not like to say no.
- Orderliness is not a prerequisite for them to be productive.
- Happy to help and support others.
- Are stressed out by any lack of harmony and balance.
- Want to be appreciated.
- For them, success is associated with how much they support other people.
- View every good relationship they form as a success.
- Do not like to be the center of attention. Prefer to remain in their personal space.
- Want to know everyone's emotional needs before beginning a job.
- Meet expectations meticulously and with determination. Feel good about finishing one project before starting a new one.
- Want to do tasks their own way after the general guidelines have been set.
- Want to be seen and heard.

What Kind of Team Member Is Air?

- They are energetic, fast, and have the ability to get other people moving.
- Do not like routine.
- Excellent communication and rhetorical skills. Can overcome many problems thanks to this ability.
- Can react impetuously and regret it later. Can quickly repair broken relationships.
- Do not like authority and rules because of their love of freedom.
- When there is conflict and tension, they are able to change the mood and bring calm.
- Prefer to talk more than to listen. Cheerful and funny. Love to tell stories.
- Do not like to be excluded. Love to be with people and in social settings.
- Want to make an impact and be accepted.
- Can easily express themselves in big groups.
- Love action and working in a crowded environment
- Want to be appreciated.
- Value physical movement over sitting at a desk.
- Not interested in detail and may quickly become bored.
- Do not do well with authoritarian and nonsocial teammates.
- Their door is open to everyone. They are influential and an inspiration.
- Like to learn by doing. Learn with activities and teamwork rather than by reading books.
- Enjoy spending time with others. Untiring.
- Do not like organization. Their desk is generally messy. Prioritize tasks by how urgent they are.
- May wait until the last minute to complete a project.
- Do not discriminate between friends. The more friends they have, the happier they are.
- Forgive easily and trust quickly.
- Losing influence or being excluded is very painful.
- Want their ideas to be heard no matter how crazy they seem.
- Highly developed capacity for seeing the big picture. This ability will benefit the team.
- Are happy on a team that likes to have fun while doing their work.
- Values status and being popular.

Relationship of the Elements
With Each Other

EARTH WATER	Compatible, make steady progress, follow the rules, have team spirit, respect authority, self-disciplined, cautious, calm, unstressed, prepared, supportive, loyal, efficient, logical, patient, good listener, productive, practical, objective.
EARTH AIR	Organized, dynamic, optimistic, orderly, cautious, inspiring, analytical, balanced, trustworthy.
EARTH FIRE	Organized, systematic, logical, analytical, see the big picture, courageous, reliable, confident, competitive, direct
AIR FIRE	Energetic, optimistic, charitable, persuasive, funny, emotional, exciting, supportive, faithful, creative, act quickly, transparent communicators, visible, diplomatic, adapt easily, friendly, peacemaker
WATER FIRE	Results-oriented, quick, cautious, flexible, straightforward, transforming, rhythmic, humane, warm
AIR WATER	Take action quickly, motivating, inspirational, love control, love change, impatient, responsible, initiators, passionate, optimistic, risk-taking, visionary, creative

Relationship Of The Elements
With Each Other

Purpose: The bodily expression of every element is different. Recognizing these expressions will help us ensure balance. When we are in balance, we are fully connected with the earth, and we can take full advantage of the four elements.

Duration: 25 minutes

Materials: A spacious area that allows freedom of movement. Everyone chooses a partner to work with on this activity.

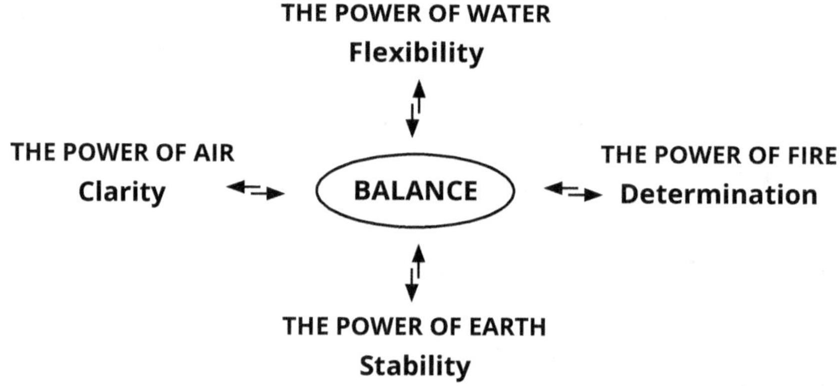

Fire

In this exercise, fire is expressed as *determination*. This is the energy of a samurai, or a mother fighting for her children, or a project manager who continues to direct his team forward in spite of setbacks. With determination, people dedicate themselves to a more important purpose or outcome, and risk their ego, identity, security, or future for the sake of this purpose.

A determined personality generally experiences fear or anxiety, but dares to courageously move forward.

Physical Exercise for Fire

Purpose: To reach the goal.

Right now, you are focused on a goal, and you are bravely moving toward that goal. You are extremely motivated and totally concentrated. You have locked on to the target in the true sense of the word. You are filled with excitement and courageously tackling every obstacle you encounter. You have put yourself out there, taken the initiative, and are moving forward.

What does the power of fire feel like in your body? In what part of your body is this feeling concentrated?

Earth

In this exercise, earth is expressed as *stability*. It is stamina, tranquility, and security. It is the energy required to maintain calm in times of crisis. The message here is this: "I am calm, and my feet are planted firmly on the ground. I am as solid as a rock." It is the energy of a leader that has total command of what he is doing and all the details, a leader that is resolved and does not lose this secure footing come what may.

Physical Exercise for Earth

Purpose: Order, clarity, justice, setting boundaries and protecting them.

You maintain your composure no matter what is happening around you. Feel your feet touching the ground. As you stand there, feel your backbone connect with the earth. Bend your knees slightly. Breathe from your abdomen. Your stance is like a rock gripped by the earth. Nothing can knock you down. You know this, which inspires confidence in those around you. You are aware of every detail and have calculated all the risks. You know there will be no surprises. Your stance is clear and strong. Everything is going as planned.

What does the power of earth feel like in your body? In what part of your body is this feeling concentrated?

Air

In this exercise, air is expressed as *clarity*. With clarity, a person makes others a partner in their own dreams. It is the energy we use to persuade others. The foundation here is connecting and succeeding with others. It is "Us." It is the energy of close friends and successful teams.

Physical Exercise for Air

Purpose: Moving in tandem.

You are having an enjoyable conversation with the people around you. You hear and see them. You are happy to be together and to be communicating. You are generating ideas. You say, "Come with me," as you invite others to join your dream. You are in high spirits. There is a big, beautiful smile on your face.

What does the power of air feel like in your body? In what part of your body is this feeling concentrated?

Water

In this exercise, water is expressed as *flexibility*. Flexibility means flowing like water, not avoiding new experiences, and being adaptable. It is possible to expand boundaries by being flexible. It is the energy required to try something before making a decision so that one can make extraordinary decisions. People can only acquire brand-new experiences when they can be flexible and are able to leave their comfort zones. It is the energy used by inventors, visionaries, and those who use their creativity.

Physical Exercise for Water

Purpose: To gain experience and get out of comfort zones.

Imagine that you have left a cage and now have freedom of movement. You can go any direction and try every possibility. You can go quickly or slowly in a relaxed or exuberant fashion. You can float in the air like steam or become ice and experience stillness. You can be a quiet brook or a raging river. Imagine that you are a dry leaf on the water and that you are flowing with it. You have surrendered yourself and are open to all possibilities. You are waiting expectantly for what will happen. A voice inside your head is saying, "Don't be afraid to try."

What does the power of water feel like in your body? In what part of your body is this feeling concentrated?

Discussion Time

Which element did you feel most comfortable working with? Which one was difficult for you? How did your language change as your body expressed the different elements?

ACTIVITY

Knowing Ourselves as a Team

Purpose: To be aware of the different personality characteristics on the team and to see all of the team's characteristics.

Duration: 10 minutes.

Materials: Adhesive tape, element symbols, notepad, and pen.

The room is divided into four equal areas by making a "+" symbol with tape on the floor. The members of the group are asked to position themselves on the element for which they scored highest on the personality test they have already taken.

The groups gathered on the same element are asked this question: How does it make you feel to be here?

Then, the situation is evaluated in terms of team integrity. These questions will be answered:

Which element is most prevalent on the team? What advantage does this offer?

Which element is rarer? What disadvantage results from this?

What would be different if you were to bring more of this element to the team?

Element Test

How Strong Are You In Your Element?

This test was developed to help you identify and understand your characteristic behaviors.

The aim of this test is to identify your style based on behavioral indicators and situational behavior analysis. In order for the test to achieve its purpose, it is critical that you answer all the questions transparently and truthfully. Therefore, you need to specify your real attitudes and not the attitudes you want to have or think you should have.

None of the four main styles that determine behavioral style indicate any right approach. All of the styles have pluses and minuses. In other words, there is no absolute right answer on the test questions. The right answer varies from person to person. The purpose of the test is to identify the characteristics that express you best, and to illuminate the areas in which you need to improve so that you can achieve balance in your behavioral style, so that you are more productive in your personal and professional life.

After answering all of the questions, please add up the number of answers given to the A–B–C–D choices and enter these numbers in the section at the bottom of the test.

For the questions on the following pages, circle the answer that describes you best.

Choose the word that describes you best from among the following descriptors.

1. A) Faithful
    B) Bossy
    C) Enthusiastic
    D) Detailed

2. A) Tolerant
    B) Determined
    C) Influential
    D) Cautious

3. A) Kind
    B) Stubborn
    C) Convincing
    D) Meticulous

4. A) Calm
    B) Independent
    C) Fun-loving
    D) Rule follower

5. A) Understanding
    B) Daring
    C) People-oriented
    D) Have high standards

6. A) Tender-hearted
    B) Willing to take risks
    C) Full of life
    D) Serious

7. A) Compassionate
    B) Courageous
    C) Cheerful
    D) Realistic

8. A) Emotional
    B) Persuasive
    C) Fickle
    D) Patient

9. A) Calm
    B) Exuberant
    C) Relaxed
    D) Idealistic

10. A) Tranquil
    B) Entrepreneurial
    C) Friendly
    D) Organized

11. A) Intuitive
    B) Risk-taker
    C) Talkative
    D) Intellectual

12. A) Calming
    B) Combative
    C) Motivating
    D) Perfectionist

13. A) Serenity
    B) Domination
    C) Learning
    D) Explaining

14. A) Peacemaker
    B) Determined
    C) Affectionate
    D) Systematic

15. A) Prefer what you already know
    B) Prefer quality
    C) Prefer what is stable
    D) Prefer to research

16. A) Reasonable
    B) Strong
    C) Supportive
    D) Meticulous

17. A) Free
    B) Brave
    C) Sacrificial
    D) Fair

18. A) At peace with yourself
    B) Ambitious
    C) Jovial
    D) Innovative

19. A) Humble
    B) Self-confident
    C) Generous
    D) Principled

20. A) Flexible
    B) Uncomfortable with change
    C) Easygoing
    D) Take precautions beforehand

21. A) Others are important
    B) Quick results are important
    C) Having fun is important
    D) Doing the right thing is important

22. A) Reconciliatory
    B) Entrepreneurial
    C) Well-meaning
    D) Knowledgeable

23. A) I want to make people comfortable
    B) I want to get things moving
    C) I want to attract attention
    D) I want to be understood

24. A) Intuitive
    B) Risk-taker
    C) Talkative
    D) Intellectual

25. A) Emotions are important
    B) Work is important
    C) Communication is important
    D) System is important

26. A) I want tranquility
    B) I want to be in charge
    C) I want to be appreciated
    D) I want to understand

27. A) Skeptical
    B) Vindictive
    C) Sassy
    D) Obsessive

28. A) Lazy
    B) Short-tempered
    C) Inconsistent
    D) Depressed

29. A) Pessimistic
    B) Dominant
    C) Disorganized
    D) Boring

30. A) Lack self-confidence
    B) Selfish
    C) Shrewd
    D) Critical

31. A) Cynical
    B) Self-seeking
    C) Hot-tempered
    D) Doubtful

32. A) Exasperated
    B) Harsh
    C) Erratic
    D) Slow

33. A) Anxious
    B) Impatient
    C) Panicked
    D) Distant

34. A) Feel worthless
    B) Narcissistic
    C) Self-seeking
    D) Defensive

35. A) Passive-aggressive
    B) Offensive
    C) Irritable
    D) Vengeful

36. A) Calming
    B) Impulsive
    C) Nonconforming
    D) Cold

37. A) Dreamer
    B) Know-it-all
    C) Flamboyant
    D) Stubborn

38. A) I'm emotional
    B) I don't like to be criti-
       cized
    C) I love my freedom
    D) I don't trust easily

39. A) I'm a foul-weather friend
    B) I get things moving
    C) I change things
    D) I instill confidence

40. A) I withdraw into my shell
    B) I reevaluate
    C) I have fun and let go
    D) I plan

Knowing Myself and My Team

Below please write the total number for each answer you chose.

A______________________________ (Water)
B______________________________ (Fire)
C______________________________ (Air)
D______________________________ (Earth)

If you gave 5 points to each element on this test, this indicates that you are in balance. If you gave less than 5 points to an element, it means the energy of this element is not clearly perceived from the outside. If you gave more than 5 points to an element, it means the energy of this element is dominant and observable.

ACTIVITY

Getting To Know My Teammates

Purpose: To acquire awareness of the differences between members of the team, see the importance of multiple voices and, perspectives, and to realize how differences reflect on the team.

Duration: 15 minutes.

Materials: Notepad and pen.

Paired exercise. Participants with different elements are paired up.

A guesses which element B is. B gives a fact about their element and their resulting perspectives. A describes how they see this element in B and how they are affected by it. Swap roles after five minutes. In the last three minutes, they discuss how their own elements reflect on the team and how they are affected by the team.

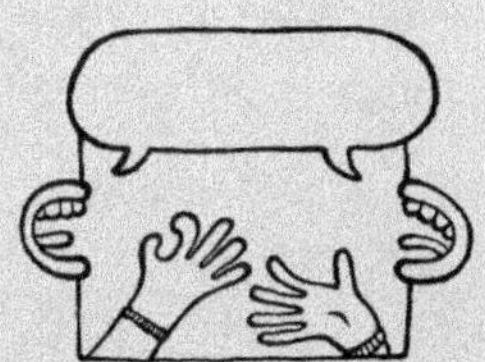

Discussion Time

Experience acquired in accepting different perspectives is shared. There is a discussion of how the experience here can be implemented in daily life.

3   TEAM COACHING SKILLS

Team Coaching Skills: Effective Listening

"Daddy, you're a coach but you don't listen to me!" I really don't know how to describe what I felt when I heard those words. Was it shock? A blow to my ego?

Erim was about 15–16 years old at the time. Because he was studying abroad, he was more comfortable expressing himself in English. Back then we had extraordinarily little time together, so I was profoundly affected by the possibility that I might be spending time with him but not listening. And for whatever reason, whether it was my need to defend myself or the desire to be a good father, I reacted immediately with the following reflexive response: "Where do you get an idea like that, son? I am here, and you have my full attention!" Erim's response was lightning fast as well. "You are listening to me, but what you are paying attention to and looking at is the little blue-and-white fishing boat there on the sea, Daddy."

I was profoundly impacted the first time I saw the Chinese symbol that expresses the verb "to listen." It consists of five main points: eye, ear, heart, mind, and undivided attention! If one of these is missing, you are not listening. You are just waiting for your turn to speak.

Listening is one of the most fundamental aspects of communication and a vital element of empathic communication. Hearing the person across from us is not enough. To be an effective listener, we must understand what they are saying and consider it. The act of listening is clearly no easy task.

Talking is a necessity, listening is an art.
—Johann Wolfgang von Goethe

Listening means giving our full attention to what is being said and understanding it. Figuring out what the person across from us is feeling will help us evaluate them and our relationship better. Misunderstandings and poorly communicated messages result in an unnecessary waste of time, a decrease in efficiency, and demoralization. Real listening is not just "being present" but being "together" with the narrator.

The process of coaching, on the other hand, requires a level of listening that is much more profound than what we employ in our daily lives. The real problem in coaching is not "listening versus not listening." The real problem is what we are focusing our attention on and the impact this has. The quality of listening and focus ensures that the coachee not only feels heard but feels as if they are in this thing together with the person who is supporting them.

During the process of communication, it is critical that there be a receptive person that can receive, decode, and evaluate the message of the sender. Communication is constructive when the receiver accurately assesses the verbal and nonverbal cues from the transmitter to access the intended meaning. The receiver is the listener.

When viewed from the four fundamental perspectives of our coaching approach, namely Me-You-We-All of Us, we see that we can base different types of listening on these fundamentals.

1. Internal Listening: The focus is on "ME." The listener is focused on their own stories, ideas, desires, emotions, and judgments. The listener is listening to their own inner voice.

2. Focused Listening: The "YOU" approach is a listening model that can be felt intensely. A laser-sharp focus from the coach to the coachee is obvious. The attention is solely one-way. Focused listening must be done well to achieve maximum success in the coaching process. Only then can we move on to higher levels of listening.

3. Systemic Listening: This is focused on "WE." As a leader or as a coach, you need to be aware of the dynamics between you and the other(s). When two or more of you get together, a theme always comes alive among you. It requires awareness to witness the hidden dynamics in the team.

4. Integral Listening: This is focused on "ALL of US." This is a level of focused listening that encompasses everything. The person will feel the energy that surrounds them. Coaches use the integral listening approach to gather more information.

For effective listening, try to listen to the person you are talking to with not only your mind but your entire body. Hear the internal voices. This will rescue you from the trap of thinking, and you will feel a unique void.

In this place, there are no thoughts or judgments to divide or distract you. As a result, you will have created a void for the narrator to occupy and express themselves. Effective listening is critical in terms of team management and leadership.

As a Team Coach, you must be on the same frequency as the emotions of the person you are dealing with. If people feel like they are really being listened to, they open up.

In order to listen effectively to the communication on the team as a Team Coach:

1. **Stay Focused:** Give your full attention to what the person across from you is saying and to the message they are trying to communicate.

2. **Give Feedback/Feedforward:** You can communicate that you are interested in the team with encouraging words, body language, questions, and summaries.

3. **Filter:** Extract your own meaning from your team members' comments and convey that. Combine your own experience, knowledge, and perception with the comments of the person talking about the issue.

Team leaders have to connect with their team and themselves. If they don't know their team's strengths and weaknesses, they cannot hand off responsibilities to the team. And if they don't know their own strengths and weaknesses, they will not hand off responsibilities to the team.
—John C. Maxwell

In order to know himself, those he interacts with and his team, a team leader needs to understand not only effective listening but also what it means to be able to look at an individual on a systems level. A systems-level view is a whole consisting of four levels. We can describe these levels as follows:

I. A Person's Inner World	• "What" and/or "How" are they thinking in the critical events they encounter? • How do they give meaning to their present experience with the stories they bring from the past?
II. Interpersonal Relationships	• "How" do they respond to others in one-on-one relationships? • What kind of response do they receive from others in one-on-one relationships? • In what way are perceptions influenced by "How" and "Where" communication occurs?
III. Group	• "How" do they respond to group members when there are differences of opinion, when problems arise, and in the different situations that occur in the group? • What is their perception of the group they are in?
IV. Organization	• How does the organization that they are a member of respond when there are differences of opinion, when problems arise, and in the different situations that occur in the organization?

ACTIVITY

Tell Me a Story

Purpose: Learning to listen to team members effectively and to view the team as a system.

Duration: 20 minutes.

Materials: Notepad and pen.

A tells B a story about themselves. B listens. The leader stops after one minute and asks B what they heard. B explains this to A.

A continues telling B the story from where they left off. B listens to A, seeking answers to the following questions:

- "What" and/or "how" are they thinking in the critical events they encounter?
- How do they give meaning to their present experience with the stories they relate from the past?
- How do they perceive and judge themselves?

A continues telling B their story. B listens to A, seeking answers to the following questions:

- "How" do they respond to others in one-on-one relationships?
- What kind of response do they receive from others in one-on-one relationships?
- In what way are perceptions influenced by "how" and "where" communication occurs.

A continues telling B their story. B listens to A, seeking answers to the following questions:

- How do they respond to members of the group when there are differences of opinion, when problems arise, and in the different situations that occur within the group?

What is their perception of the group they are in? Later, A and B will switch places.

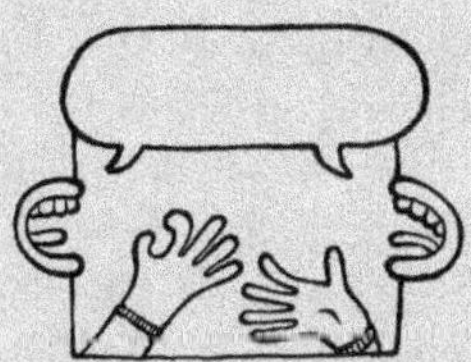

Discussion Time

How does sharing things you learn affect focused listening?
What is the effect of giving feedback?

Team Coaching Skills: Building Trust

The coaching relationship is more powerful than either the coach or the coachee. This relationship is one that motivates and encourages the coachee while pushing them toward competition and encouraging them to be strong. This relationship is independent of the coach or the coachee and is based on a foundation of trust. When the coachee and the coach trust one another, a powerful bond is formed. Remember, everyone forms trust in their own unique way. Trying to force the issue of building trust is a completely different issue. People who try to persuade others that they are trustworthy create apprehension in the people they interact with, which can keep the bond from forming.

Managing people is essentially managing their emotions, which requires that they first understand, identify, and be capable of expressing their own emotions. As a result, a person becomes aware of how the various emotions they experience affect their behavior. The coach must be aware of his or her emotions and, if they conclude it does not serve the coaching session, be more intentional about the emotional context and how to adopt emotions and behaviors that are more conducive to building trust and active listening.

The Team Coach must get out of the way in order to remain faithful to the team's agenda. It is the skill of managing oneself in order to set aside one's own personal views, preferences, pride, defense mechanisms and ego. The Team Coach must be on the same side as the team. Managing oneself means letting go of the desire to look good to others and be right. This is how coaches model the ability to manage the ideas and judgments of others and themselves.

"With so much work to do in the department and a huge backlog of work, I cannot for the life of me understand why we spend half a day sitting here. Besides, our team is doing simply fine anyway! No one has problems with anyone else. Just last week, we all had dinner with a colleague who is leaving. We laughed and had a great time." The person who said these things was the oldest and loudest member of a large team, and he was touching on an important point. In the last 18 months, 12 people had left the 23-person team or had left for a new position in another department. This means a personnel turnover of approximately 52 percent. Just then, a team member sitting nearby said in a very calm but resolved tone, "You are right, of course. We talk about little unimportant things or have short personal chats, but if it is a situation where we expect work from each other or which directly affects the success of the team, we either make a joke of it, or we talk about it with each other in the corridor instead of talking to the person involved. There is something out of whack here, Ali. If we acknowledge this, then we will have taken the first step."

The goal of every leader and team coach is a team that moves ahead by supporting each other and holds each other accountable in a constructive way for the sake of a common goal. The first step to achieving this is to create an atmosphere of trust between all of the team members.

Building Trust on Teams

A Team Coach begins his work by building trust on the team. The first breakdown on a team is the lack of trust between team members. This is basically due to the fact that they do not want to be left defenseless. Team members who are not truly transparent with one another about their mistakes and weaknesses cannot lay the foundation required for trust.

Even though trust is an abstract and intangible concept, the results are extremely concrete and tangible. Distrust has truly devastating consequences. But when there is trust, work is accomplished much more quickly.

There are three fundamental advantages to building trust:

- Not feeling the need to be defensive with each other
- Knowing that the information you provide will not be used against you
- Living without fear of being hurt

Trust is an essential part of a functioning and effective team. Without trust, teamwork is inconceivable. Many employees in the business world distance themselves from others with a shield of politeness and kindness. This avoids any appearance of conflict, and everybody appears to be getting along because no one holds anyone accountable when things go wrong, and no one is forced to give an account. These types of employees do not voice their opinion in meetings, but they also do not make any contribution to the decisions reached in meetings. The reason is simple. It is easier and more comfortable to just talk behind people's backs about the decision. Talking about other people's mistakes makes people feel better about themselves and gives them a feeling of superiority.

However, when a team builds trust, the members of the team do not doubt the good intentions of their colleagues and are not afraid of being hurt. When there is trust between team members, they do not feel the need to defend themselves.

If team members can say what they feel without hesitation, they do not worry about protecting themselves. Instead of playing politics, they are able to focus all their energy and attention on their work.

It is difficult to achieve a level of trust where one does not feel the need to defend themselves. Most successful people learn to compete, and they learn to protect themselves as they train and move ahead in their career. Letting go of this instinctive behavior for the good of the team is difficult, but essential.

Teams that are unable to create this atmosphere expend needless energy while avoiding the risk of asking for help or rendering aid to others.

Managers in most organizations only address the issue of trust when a problem arises, but by then the damage has already been done. Employees withhold information and data, managers set confusing goals, it becomes impossible to access managers, people start talking behind each other's backs, and this list just gets longer and longer.

Corporate transformation specialist Cynthia Olmstead lists some of the most common "trust breakers": broken promises, unethical behavior, unfair practices (such as undeserved promotions), failure to achieve expected results, poor communication, not being appreciated, lack of feedback/feedforward, and failure to accurately represent their areas of expertise.

Team Members without Trust

- Hide their weaknesses and mistakes from each other.
- Avoid asking for help or making constructive contributions.
- Are not open to support outside of the area they are responsible for.
- When it comes to the intentions and abilities of others, they reach conclusions without trying to understand the situation.
- Make no attempt to utilize the skills and experience of others.
- Spend time and energy on acts meant to influence their circle.
- Hold grudges.
- Avoid meetings, get bored, and make excuses for not spending time together.

Team Members with Trust

- Accept their weaknesses and mistakes.
- Ask for help.
- Are open to questions and contributions related to the area they are responsible for.
- Listen to the person they are interacting with before reaching a negative conclusion.
- Are willing to provide information and assistance.
- Appreciate the knowledge and skills of others and take advantage of them.
- Spend their time and energy on important matters.
- Apologize without hesitation and give others the opportunity to do the same.
- Look forward to meetings and teamwork.

In order to build the kind of trust that eliminates the need to protect oneself, there must be shared experiences over time with various activities conducted together and a proper understanding of both trustworthiness and the unique abilities of the different team members.

Trust is essentially a verbal or nonverbal promise and commitment. When we trust people, we show them our true self. The relationship between the coach and the team is an incredibly special relationship. It is essential that the right emotional atmosphere is created in order to successfully implement the program. Therefore, a relationship of trust must be built between the Team Coach and the team. This is like the foundation of a building. In order to have a strong building, it is critical that the foundation be strong. The same is true of trust in relationships. When the boundaries are clearly defined, trust is extremely easy to build.

In order to define these boundaries, the team and the Team Coach must answer questions like the following:

- Who?
- What responsibility?
- For how long?

It has been demonstrated that relationships with clearly defined boundaries based on reciprocal trust are healthier and last longer.

Even if the team does build trust in the short term with these tools and activities, constant monitoring is required during daily activities. Personal development plans must be reviewed, without sacrificing momentum. Regression can occur even on a strong team, and this can have a negative effect on trust.

The more pressure the Team Coach puts on team members to compete, the less trust there will be on the team because team members will want to be number one. The team must transition from applauding individual accomplishment to cheering for team accomplishments.

In order to build trust, it is important that as the Team Coach you demonstrate that no one on the team has to fear being hurt. This means you have to risk losing prestige with the team. As a result, team members will be able to take the same risk. It is extremely difficult for people to acknowledge their weaknesses and failures. On teams that have built trust, people can be real about themselves without being defensive.

It is important that a team make conflict possible by creating trust because only then can the team members stop avoiding heated and sometimes emotional discussions, since they know that what they say will not be interpreted as just being critical or hurtful.

Cultivating the art of having "difficult conversations" in which people may not agree or when interpretations of a situation are very different raises the dilemma of "who is right" or "who has the authority to decide future action." Being heard doesn't mean that one's idea is adopted. Somewhere in all of this is the notion of acceptance for different points of view as enriching to the team's intelligence. And there are typically certain people who have the deciding vote on what strategy will be followed. How the contribution of ideas or perceptions can be constructive is an open question for all team members. Diversity strengthens the range of possibilities to act.

As the amount of sharing between team members increases and they get to know each other better, they will develop more sincerity and stronger bonds. It is important that the Team Coach facilitate this bonding process.

SIDEBAR

Practical Methods for the Team Coach: Trust-Building Exercises

Exercise 1: A "Personal History Exercise" can be conducted by asking members questions about themselves in any meeting or whenever they spend time together. For example, asking harmless questions like where they were born, number of children, challenges faced in childhood, their favorite hobbies, their first job, or the worst job they ever had can bring team members closer and encourage them to have personal relationships. As a result, team members will realize how little they know about each other or that their opinions are wrong. It is sometimes very surprising for people who have been together for a long time to realize how little they know about each other.

Exercise 2: Even though it seems more difficult than the previous exercise, the "Team Activity Exercise" is an effective one. In order to do this, team members need to know what their most important contribution to the group is as well as what they need to improve or give up for the benefit of the team.

All members will express their opinions about every other member of the team, usually starting with the Team Coach. It does not take long to see how effective this exercise is at eliciting constructive and positive information.

Exercise 3: Effective and more time-consuming steps can be taken to build trust by identifying the personality profiles and behavioral preferences of the team members. This helps them get to know each other better and removes obstacles to them getting closer. At this point, the results of in-house tools can also be used.

Exercise 4: Information sharing. Team members can share specific information with each other. This type of sharing helps build trust on the team. Here are some possible subjects: work done by the competition, future strategies and business plans, financial data, industry-specific topics and problematic departments, competitor practices worthy of consideration, ways to achieve organizational objectives through teamwork, performance feedback/feedforward.

Exercise 5: Making apology tours. Apologizing and correcting mistakes is an effective way to rebuild the trust required for good relationships. However, in many organizations, employees and managers tend to hide mistakes because they think that they will not be met with an understanding attitude. The result is that problems get even bigger. Setting aside some team time and creating an environment where every member can apologize or confess mistakes can build a lot of trust on the team. It is extremely important for trust to foster an attitude that can be summarized as, "Anyone can make a mistake. We are a team; we will handle this among ourselves. Let's just be transparent with one another."

Exercise 6: The Team Coach can, during important times, ask that team members complete some unfinished sentences. Several different sentences like those below can be constructed:

My trust in this team...

I wish that I could do or say... on this team.

What I trust about this team is...

I want to thank the team I am part of for...

What do I need to trust my colleague or my boss?

Working to Strengthen the Bond between Team Members

Sharing Stages of Life

In his stages of psychosocial development, Erik Erikson described the different stages of life as a process that encompasses the development of self throughout all of human experience. According to him, the self goes through various stages of development, solves problems and tries to overcome the crisis resulting from the characteristics of each stage. We have a different view of life during each biological phase. The philosophy of each stage is different. The stages of life are associated both with personal and social development; this is the pathway to life. These stages have been described as:

1. **First 9 months: MOTHER'S WOMB (Fetus) — Awareness of Unity**
   Fundamental outcome: Hope
   Most important relationship: Mother
   Conflict of this stage: Can I trust the world?

   This stage is based on following Mom in the manner life itself has determined. This is a physiological, psychological and existential stage. The child is completely nourished by the emotions it feels from its mother. External factors are filtered through Mom and reflected to the child.

2. **Up until the age of 10: CHILDHOOD — We (Group) Awareness**
   Fundamental outcome: Competence
   Most important relationship: Family, relatives, friends
   Conflict of this stage: Is it acceptable for me to do this?
   Can I do this in society?

This stage represents compulsion and identity, trust, stability/unreliability, family values, religion, traditions and customs, collective conscience, blind love and childishness.

3. Up until the age of 20: ADOLESCENCE — Awareness of Ego
Fundamental outcome: Fidelity
Most important relationship: Role models
Conflict of this stage: Who am I? What could I be?

This is the most difficult stage, representing rebellion, a desire for self-actualization, the first feeling of ego and its fragmentation, experiencing and living everything, unlimited desires, action, control, power, and the fact that the order of life is threatened. This is where ego becomes settled. The young person is presented with two tasks.
- Leaving their family; in other words, finding themselves and
- finding their place in society.

4. Up until the age of 30: YOUNG ADULT — Awareness of Dependence
Fundamental outcome: Love
Most important relationship: Friends, lover
Conflict of this stage: Can I love?

This is the stage that represents being one's own person, sharing, love, sexuality and trust. Being an adult is not holding other people responsible for your actions and the consequences of those actions. The essence of adulthood is meeting your own needs.

5. Age 30-60: MATURE ADULTHOOD — Awareness of Transfer (Expression)
Fundamental outcome: Care
Most important relationship: Home life and colleagues
Conflict of this stage: Can I make my life valuable?

This is the stage of vision. During this time, perception becomes clearer. Life begins taking a definite direction, for which approval can be given. This is called vision.

6. **Over 60: OLD AGE — Awareness of Integrity**
Fundamental outcome: Wisdom
Most important relationship: Humanity
Conflict of this stage: Was it good being "Me"?

We see that all of the mistakes made up until this point were part of the journey and that birth and death are on equal footing. We know that we have come to where we are because of what we have lived through and that other people need to make these mistakes too. We also know that everyone is destined to live what they experience.

ACTIVITY

I Share The Turning Points In My Life

Purpose: To boost sincerity and bonding on the team, allow participants to experience how sharing can transform the atmosphere and how to use creative channels.

Step 1: The participants are divided into groups of five. Each participant is given materials to make their own collage (A3 paper, magazines, glue). Participants make a collage to depict their own life stages, starting with adolescence, and featuring the events they consider turning points in these stages. They are given 10 minutes for the collage. Then, each participant presents their work to their group for 5 minutes.

Step 2: A joint collage project for the team.
The team makes a collage of their history up until the present time.

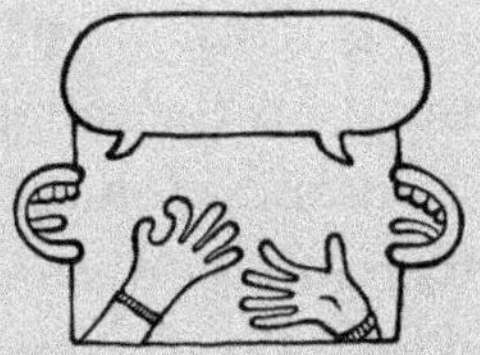

Discussion Time

The team members share and assess their awareness regarding issues like bonding and building trust.

Team Coaching Skills: Observation

The Journey from My Values to Our Values

Ayesha had been working as an executive in an information technology company for six years. We had only been working together for two weeks, and she was in the middle of a challenging project with her team, almost half of whom were new members. Her first words were, "The truth is I really never thought it could be this effective." I was taken aback by the statement and asked, "That what could be effective?" She heard the question but was so focused on what she was going to say that she ignored it and continued. "You know that we are trying to successfully wrap up this project we started last year. It has presented both financial and administrative challenges as we face a number of limitations resulting from both our own lack of experience and external factors. And no matter how hard we tried, things just kept going wrong." She took a breath and then added. "Our last project meeting started just like always—what was missing, identifying the problems, the mistakes we had made, how we would correct them, etc. And this time, instead of getting tangled up in the issues and events, I was able to remain on the outside as I had resolved to do in our last conversation and look at issues like "What kind of dynamic is being created on the team? What are we doing? What is our dialogue like? Who is participating in the conversation? Who is watching from the sidelines?"

I was moved by the excitement in Ayesha's voice. I said, "You are so enthusiastic and happy. In fact, you have been smiling this whole time. I am really curious. What kind of effect did this experience have on you and your team?" She answered without hesitation: "I realized that we had utilized very little of our resources, that the new members of the team were not really clued in to our primary objective, that we were not really a team focused on a common goal, but more like a group of people running around putting out fires. Now, I can see more clearly where we need to start. ... The most urgent and logical thing to do is build a team..." It's true. We do not become a team just by being in the same room. We are just a group of people, and in order to connect the ground under our feet with the ground others are standing on, to form a partnership, and realize where we are, it is critical that we each take a step back and just observe, both in our work and in our private lives.

How can I unleash the "amazing me," the "motivated me" trapped inside? What is hindering me?

Personal and collective motivations and what is important constitute a person's values. These could be love, success, freedom, responsibility, excellence, closeness, health, security, ambition, comfort, etc.

Values exist whether or not one is aware of them. Tension is created when there is conflict between values and reality.

According to Tony Robbins, giving something value is essentially saying that it is important. Everything you love is actually a value. Your values affect your life journey. When you are aware of your values, you are aware of the path you are following in life. Being aware of your own values clarifies why you do what you do, and helps you live more consistently.

People who know their own values and live accordingly can become the leader of their group because every decision is based on clarification of values.

When you live in accordance with your values, life is an easy and delightful journey. When a list emerges of what makes a person an individual and what their nonnegotiables are, it becomes easier to make decisions and act. Therefore, everyone should find the answers to the following questions:

- What are your fundamental rules and principles? In a sense, what is your constitution?
- What values could you never abandon?
- How do you feel if you compromise your values?
- After identifying your fundamental principles, you will have an amazing guide to use for decision-making and planning. Maybe even a compass. How far off course does your compass say you are sometimes? When that happens, what happens to you? How do you feel? What do you need to do to get back on course?

The principal duty of a team leader is to manage team values. The most effective way to motivate people is to satisfy their needs.

The most important values that people have are always a reflection of their stage of psychological development. Our basic needs are at the top of this list. Your needs always shape your behavior and activities and will continue to do so.

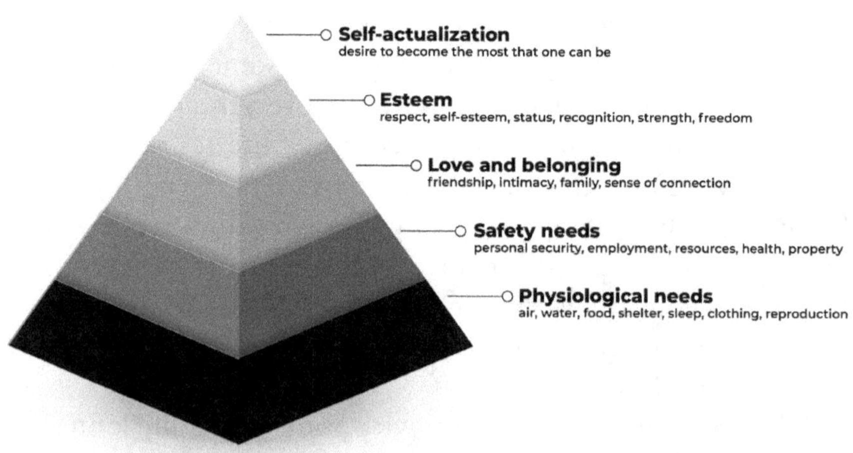

According to the renowned psychologist Abraham Maslow, until an individual has satisfied the more basic instincts, they are not affected by the higher instincts. When the more basic needs are satisfied, an individual is ready for the higher-level needs.

Happiness can only blossom when basic needs are satisfied. However, if these needs are threatened (thinking about the possibility of losing a job or friends, or that people do not respect you), the result is fear and anxiety.

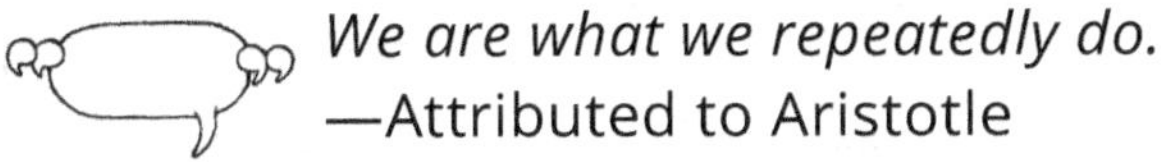 *We are what we repeatedly do.*
—Attributed to Aristotle

When people understand themselves, it is possible to satisfy development needs. When a person truly reaches a place where they can give meaning to who they are, they discover their true self, their soul. They find the meaning and purpose of life. Pleasure and satisfaction occur when a person's developmental needs are met.

The way to achieve long-lasting happiness is to live according to high ideals, and to live a life that is consistent with what we believe about life. Therefore, one must determine what is important in life. A person who does not clearly know what their values are cannot achieve long-lasting happiness. Many people know what they want to have but do not know who they want to be. Remember that material possessions alone do not satisfy a person. Identifying your values and doing only what you believe is right is the way to personal satisfaction.

According to Ken Wilber's four quadrants, personality, character, culture and social structure are positioned as follows:

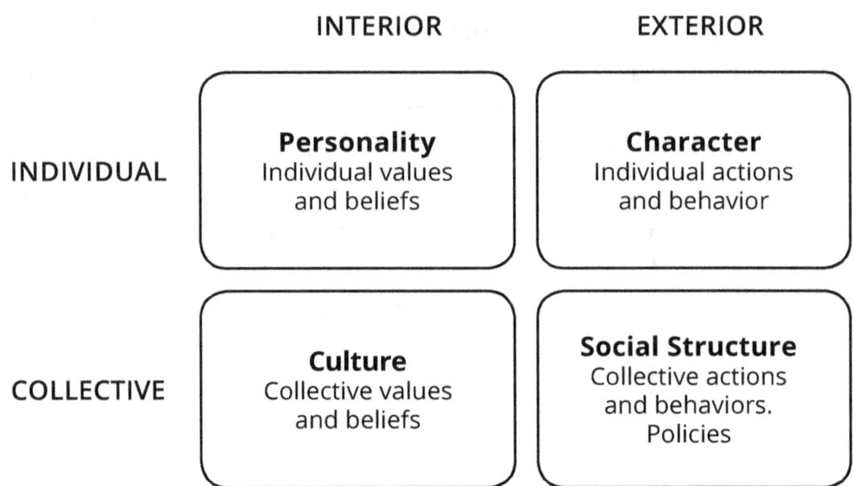

The four quadrants, which are four basic perspectives in any situation or four basic ways of looking at any issue, become quite simple: the interior and exterior of an individual and society. In the upper-left quadrant (the individual's interior structure, "me"), you can see your thoughts, feelings, sensations, etc. The upper-right quadrant is how the event looks from the outside. All of these are things that we can describe as an objective third party or "it." Every "me" is in relationship with the other me's, and this means that every "me" is a member of the various "we" groups. These "we" groups represent not only individual but also collective awareness.

This is shown in the lower-left quadrant. The lower-left quadrant is called the cultural dimension (or the group's internal awareness, worldview, shared values, shared feelings, etc.). Similarly, every "we" has an exterior structure or an aspect that is visible from the outside, and this forms the lower-right quadrant. The lower-right quadrant is the social dimension. Healthy communication takes all four quadrants into account.

The quadrants constitute the interior and exterior aspects of the individual and society, and the important thing is to include all four quadrants as much as possible.

Personal transformation in leaders is the beginning of transformation on teams. This is also the only way to change the system as a whole because organizations do not implement change, but rather the individuals inside the organization.

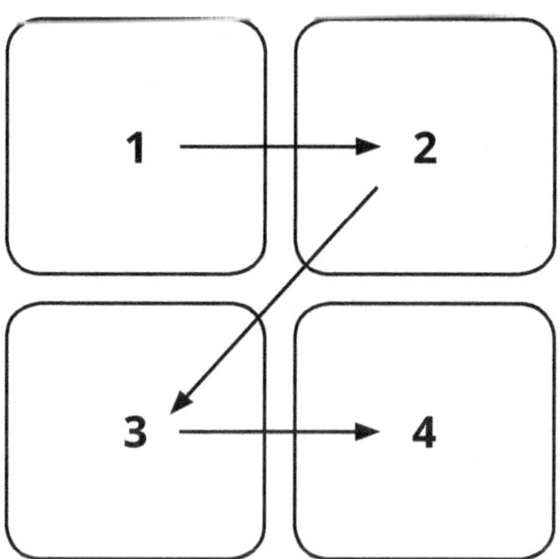

When they (1) change their beliefs and values, (2) leaders change their behavior, (3) which affects group culture, (4) resulting in changing the behavior of the group.

As we see, one person changing their values can change the entire organization. The flow of life is influenced by the magnetism of values. They are the force field of our lives. Individuals direct their lives based on values, thereby determining the destination at which they hope to arrive. Remember that values are the compass that will move a person/organization toward their final destiny.

The job of a Team Coach is to shed light on the team's shared values. The team members must first become aware of their own values and then reach an agreement about the common values they identify for the team.

The coach must have highly developed observational skills in this process of identifying values. Careful observation is a very important coaching competency. The best coaching interventions occur by observing behaviors, patterns, changes in tone of voice, pace of the conversation, gestures, and interactions.

At this point, it is essential that our preconceived ideas be set aside and that we observe the situation objectively. A person must raise their own awareness. It is also impossible to be neutral when one's emotions, anger, or surprise affect the observation.

The first step in effective Team Coaching is to understand the situation, the person and their current skill set. The best way to do this is through observation. Our goal should be to identify that person's strengths and weaknesses and to understand the effect that their behavior has both on their teammates and on their ability to achieve their own goals.

During observation, keep the following in mind:

- By definition, observation is inherently a world of interpretation, assessments, and yes, judgments. By observing, we are assessing the people and situations through our own worldview, emotions, and honest blind spots.
- Figure out what the person does well and what they are unable to do. To the extent possible, reach clear and definitive conclusions, and try to understand the reason for the problems.
- Avoid passing judgment too soon. Observing once or twice will not give you a good understanding of the situation. Therefore, continue observing, especially if you have doubts about the ideas you have formed.
- Test your theories. Discuss the matter with your colleagues in appropriate situations. Take their observations into account as well.
- Avoid unrealistic expectations. Assuming that the team members have motivations and strengths similar to yours may not be realistic and it may result in an unfair approach.
- Listen carefully. Someone may want your help, but you may not be able to hear them. Ask yourself if you have missed opportunities to listen. People may not always know exactly what kind of help they need or how to ask for it. When you have an opportunity, make time to actively listen to team members and direct them.

- Discuss your observations with the team. Talk about the behavior you have observed. Discuss the impact that the behavior of individuals has on team objectives and colleagues. When describing this behavior and its impact, be sincere and honest, but also supportive. Do not let the discussion venture into reasons for the behavior. Otherwise, you will cause the person to feel like they are being personally attacked. If you talk about the reasons for the behavior, you will just be speculating.

ACTIVITY

Identifying my Values and Those of the Team: Attributes

Purpose: Developing the skills of listening and observing while identifying the values of participants.

Duration: 40 minutes.

Materials: List of values, notepad, pen.

Paired exercise. A and B will work together to answer the following questions.

Step 1:

- Which of the values on the list below characterize you best?
- Which of the values on the list below best characterize how your team operates?
- Which of the values on the list below would you like to see on your team?

Ambition/Passion	Cooperation
Balance (career/personal life)	Courage
Being a listener	Creating distinction
Being able to forgive	Dedication
Being liked	Determination/resolve
Being noticed	Eco-friendliness
Being the best	Efficiency
Clarity	Enthusiasm
Compassion	Entrepreneurship
Compatibility	Ethics
Competency	Excellence

Fairness	Patience
Family	Peace-making
Financial stability	Personal development
Freedom	Personal satisfaction
Friendship	Power/strength
Future generations	Professional development
Generosity	Prudence (being cautious)
Healthy life	Recognition
Honesty	Respect
Humility	Responsibility/accountability
Humor/fun	Safety
Image	Self-Discipline
Initiative	Success
Job security	Support
Leadership	Taking risks
Learning	The unknown
Loyalty to the community	Transparency
Mercy	Trustworthiness

Questions:

- What are the values that make you who you are?
- With which values do you support the team?
- What are the values you use the most or not at all? What would be possible if you used them more?
- What value does the team use the most or not use at all?

Step 2: List the three most important values you chose for yourself.

1.
2.
3.

- Why are these values important for you?
- Think of a time when you fully implemented these values in your life. How did you act?
- How do you act when others do not respect these values of yours?

Team Coaching Skills: Asking Powerful Questions

It's been said, "You understand a person's intelligence not from the answers they give, but from the questions they ask." However, we have been taught since we were little that we will be recognized for the "answers" we give to questions. In fact, I remember how in junior high school I would raise my hand whenever the history teacher asked who wanted to explain the subject even if I did not know the subject (though I had hastily reviewed it during break). Now I am able to see more clearly how the times when I tried to be the one who knew the answers hindered me when I was working as a manager. As we all know, the executive—in today's parlance, the leader—was supposed to know everything. He never asked questions, but he knew all the answers. He was like Superman. But, of course this is not true. For a long time, I have called this being the know-it-all instead of the sage, or to be more honest, ever since I recognized my own know-it-all attitude. Whether you call them leaders or executives, when they support the team they work with as they help them move forward, find their own answers and methods and get out of their comfort zones, they are truly providing maximum benefit to both the team and the organization. To the extent that we activate the neurons in the brains of the people we work with and make it possible for them to think and forge a path, we are creating value. There is a common proverb, "Don't give a man fish but teach him to fish." As we move toward the 22nd century, I feel like this proverb is missing something. Maybe it should be, "Don't give a man fish; help him find his own way to fish."

Coaching is the art of asking the right questions. The quality of the question opens a person's mind and determines the quality of the answer. It encourages them to think about things they have never considered. Every question you ask results in the coachee challenging their assumptions and considering/seeing something they did not see before. Therefore, one of the most powerful aspects of coaching is knowing how to ask the right questions.

Asking powerful questions invites the team not to take a certain direction but to examine themselves, which offers solutions and leads to greater creativity and insight. Team awareness is raised via powerful questions and answers. Asking questions is the best way to understand the person you are interacting with and to identify their perspective. It focuses on the future and leads to a brand-new space.

A coach does not need to search for answers or know the issue in depth to ask powerful questions. That is the team's job. Really, all the coach has to do is have the curiosity of a child.

The questions asked by the coach should be open-ended, proactive and inviting. These types of questions focus the team members on a specific point. These are not the types of questions that point them in a certain direction. If the question leads to a dead-end, the coachees will realize this anyway. Then, the coach will move on to a different question.

It is exciting to examine things with curiosity. Together the coach and team members enter a void and take a look around. The result is situations where, in childlike innocence, people say, "Look what I found!" It creates a vast void that is fun and exciting.

There are several different ways of asking questions:

- Closed-ended questions
- Open-ended questions
- Deep questions
- Powerful questions
- Fact-based questions
- Cause-based questions
- Value-based questions

Be careful about using closed-ended questions. Closed-ended questions produce answers like "yes" and "no." In closed-ended questions, the answer is generally known. They are used to wrap up the past and provide direction. As the Team Coach, you can encourage everyone to be unified by asking the closed-ended question "Are we all on the same page?"

Examples: Closed-ended questions

- In order to focus the answer on a specific point: "Is the project on schedule?"
- In order to have the person you are interacting with confirm what they said: "In this case, the critical point is cost, correct?"

Ask open-ended questions. Open-ended questions encourage participation and the sharing of ideas.

When you want more information about the intentions and emotions of the team members, use open-ended questions. With these types of questions, you can elicit the real thoughts and emotions of the team you are coaching. Open-ended questions make the team feel more powerful, and they may be able to find solutions themselves by thinking more deeply about their projects. This also gives you the opportunity to formulate more effective ideas and sharing times that might help your team.

Examples: Open-ended questions

- To consider alternatives: "If this had happened, what would have been the outcome?"
- To elicit attitudes and needs: "What do you think about the progress that you have made so far?"
- To identify and consider priorities: "What do you think are the primary problems with this project?"

When the Team Coach needs to make a suggestion, proposal or comment, this can be accomplished with open-ended questions. Otherwise, discussions that have a commanding tone make the communication seem controlling and hinder the flow of ideas.

Examples: Deep questions

- What strengths do we have that will help us accomplish our objectives?
- What do we need to focus on to improve ourselves as a team?

Deep questions cannot be answered immediately. One needs time to think, observe and research in order to answer them.

The Team Coach can use powerful questions to encourage the team to think deeply and in a particular direction. You can use these types of questions to help the team find missing information about the issue they are working on or to better understand the situation they are in or the emotions they or others are experiencing.

Examples: Powerful questions

- What do we want?
- What will we gain from this?
- What is hindering us?
- What is your most powerful trait?
- What challenges are we ready to take on?
- What is the next step?
- What is another way to do it?
- Who/what can we influence?
- What is important to us?

Powerful questions

- Are open-ended.
- Focus on learning.
- Are concise and clear.
- Encourage introspection.
- Put people in the position of being creative, self-sacrificing, and taking the initiative.
- Motivate the team toward its goals instead of looking back and being right.
- Are surprising.
- Encourage people to look to the future.
- Asking powerful questions at the right point in a dialogue helps focus and enlighten the discussion so that the real issues are brought into the open.
- Help people gain the clarification they need for themselves so they can communicate their perspective.

You can ask questions from the following three basic categories to establish deeper relationships and gain greater insight.

Fact-Based Questions

These are questions about factual information asked in a conversational setting. The answers to these questions are sometimes found in personnel files.

Examples: Fact-based questions

- Where were you born?
- What kind of games did you play when you were a child?
- What was the model of your first car?
- Were you involved in any clubs in school?
- How many years have you been working here?
- Can you tell us about your family?

Cause-Based Questions

These questions are asked to determine what influenced or caused the answers given to the fact-based questions. They generally consist of "what" and "why" questions.

Examples: Cause-based questions

- Why do we need to clarify the team's award?
- Why are we solving our problem with this approach?
- What brought us where we are right now?

Value-Based Questions

These questions are the kind that help us understand the value judgments of the person we are interacting with. These questions are formulated so that the person answering the question is forced to provide the exact details we want to hear. These types of questions can on rare occasions shed light on the person's entire inner self.

Examples: Value-based questions

- Can you tell us about an accomplishment on the team that impacted you?
- If you had the chance to relive or redo something, what would you want to do differently?
- What is a source of pride for this team or its peak performance?
- What kind of advice would you give to a young person who was asking the team for guidance?

Examples of Powerful Questions

What?	What will we do? What do we want? What accomplishment would make us distinctive?
How?	How will we accomplish this? How can we focus on this issue? How can we overcome this obstacle?
Where?	Where do we want to be? Where do we see ourselves in this entire organization?
When?	When will we have accomplished this? When will we fulfill the responsibilities we assumed?
Why?	(It is recommended that these be used sparingly.) In your opinion, why are we having this problem?
Who?	Who will be responsible for this? Who will be held responsible for the decisions we make to reach our team goals and how will this be done?

Opening Questions

- What is our goal?
- In general, what motivates us?
- What do we want to be?
- What do we really want?
- What kind of impact will this have?
- What kind of result do we want?
- How will we know that we have reached our goals?
- Who else is this important to?
- How will we feel when we have achieved our goal?
- How will these things affect our life?
- What do we see in the big picture when we look at the issue from 10,000 feet?
- What else is important about this?

Detailed Questions

- What might be the best thing?
- Can you elaborate on this a little bit?
- What kind of feeling is this?
- What does this tell us?
- What do you believe is going on here? In your opinion, is this true?
- What sort of conclusion have you arrived at?
- How do you think each of us has contributed to this?
- Can you give an example?
- Can we research this a bit more?
- Like what?
- In your opinion, what other details are involved?
- What else can you tell us about this matter?

- What other details do we know about the matter?
- If we could do this over again, what would we do differently?
- If it had been you, what would you have done? What could you have done differently?
- What caused this?
- What have we tried so far?
- Do you remember how it happened?
- What do you think the chances of success are?
- What did we learn about this?
- Where is this going?
- If we do it, what will the results be?
- If we do not do it, what will the results be?
- What is our biggest obstacle?
- What is stopping us?
- What is causing the greatest problem?
- Is there anything that is perplexing to you?
- What else could we say about this matter?
- How would you describe this?
- How would you summarize our efforts up to this point? What have we done?
- What else could we have done?
- If this were a matter of life and death, what would you do?
- If you had had the opportunity to choose in this matter, what would you have chosen?
- What kind of resources do we need to help us make a decision?
- What will you do?
- What is our action plan?
- What kind of plan do we need to make?
- Which of our strengths can we leverage?
- What are our other choices?
- What can help us reach our goal?
- How will we do it?
- When will we do it?

- What will we do if the same thing happens again?
- If we were to start over, what would we do?
- What other choices do we have as possible solutions?
- How can we motivate ourselves?
- How can we stay focused?
- How can we improve this situation?

Obstacle-Awareness Questions

- What could we encounter in this process?
- Which of our habits may hold us back?
- What other issues will we face?
- What will happen if we fail to accomplish it?
- How do we address these issues?
- If things don't turn out like we hoped, what do we plan to do?
- How can we stay concentrated?

Closing Questions

- What sort of conclusion are you drawing from this?
- How can we explain this to ourselves?
- In your opinion, what was the lesson here?
- What have we learned from this process?
- When we look at all the details, what does the big picture look like?
- What is the shared takeaway from this?
- How can we explain the contribution it has made to us?

ACTIVITY

Asking Powerful Questions About Mind And Emotions

Purpose: To experience the effect of asking powerful questions.

Duration: 20 minutes.

Materials: Notepad and pen.

Form groups of five and choose a group leader. The leader will share for five minutes about whatever issue they want. For the next ten minutes, the group will ask questions. The group leader will take notes about how the questions affected him.

After ten minutes have passed, the group will spend five minutes sharing their observations and choose an area of awareness to share with the larger group.

Discussion Time

When the teamwork is completed, the information will be shared with the big group for ten minutes.

SIDEBAR

A Powerful Transition from Why to How

*This is an excerpt from an experience that professional coach
Andrew Halfacre had with a coachee.*

The source of the questions we ask ourselves may sometimes be job-related stress. Let's take a look at this issue with my new coachee John. John started work at a new company with a handsome salary. However, he was shocked to discover that the new environment had a culture that was very foreign to him.

He was complaining about how disappointed he was in the new team and talking about how they were not doing anything to implement the actions they had decided on, complaining about the company bureaucracy and how work had been done in his previous company. I realized that he was unconsciously but continually using "why" questions.

- Why aren't they listening?
- Why can't I encourage them to act?
- Why does everything take so long here?
- Why can't they see that there are better ways to work together?
- Why am I having so much trouble gaining their trust?

Remember that "why" questions lead us to aimless inquiry and create disappointment.

"How" questions are more useful.

- How can I be understood?
- How can I structure the meeting? How can I prepare so that it is easier to sell my ideas?

The question "How can I do it?" is much more effective than the question "Why is this happening?" because with "how" you retain control. Instead of trying to give meaning to problems, you focus on opportunities. These questions arouse curiosity instead of disappointment.

If you are experiencing disappointment, maybe it is time for you to ask different questions.

Team Coaching Skills: Discovering Internal Team Dynamics

In a workshop we recently conducted with the team members of an international company who were located in different countries, the team leader shared his Dialog in the Dark experience. I don't want to go into a lot of detail now and ruin the magic of this very valuable experience, but the main idea was that sometimes the information we get from our senses does not make our experience more profound but more shallow. I realized that the competitive work environment that we live in, where decisions are made or conclusions are drawn quickly, pulls me away from real contact with the person I'm interacting with.

But in fact, we are in constant communication either with ourselves or our environment. In our careers today, we are working with several different generations, often called generation X, Y, and the Internet Generation. In the 1960s, the dominant trend was to "avoid judgmental statements" and this generation was followed by the "political correctness" movement of the 1990s. The merger of the two resulted in conversations focused on "sharing" rather than on deep and serious discussion of different views.

Our tendency to avoid conflict or the efforts we make to suppress conflict not only lay the foundations for an artificial and fake environment without trust that prevents the emergence of creative ideas or genuine communication, it actually reinforces that foundation.

When we view it from this perspective, I can say from my experience on several teams I worked with that merely giving feedback does not remedy problems, and that we need other tools and areas of communication to work together successfully. We must use a wider range of skills to communicate effectively and to understand both ourselves and others. At this point, I would like to share with you some of the approaches and tools that will support your practice, but which are not what we consider mainstream.

Healthy communication between team members is essential for a team to be able to work together effectively. The foundation of team synergy is bringing people together around a specific purpose and creating unity of purpose. The synergy will be negatively affected if the team members fail to perform their duties or do not participate responsibly. Sharing and a sense of ownership between all team members will significantly enhance team performance. The formation of cliques within the team will have a negative impact on the team's performance and can increase the tendency to anarchy. This is why it is necessary to prevent the formation of cliques.

Team members may frequently experience tension with other members due to their personal beliefs. In this situation, what is right for the team may not be right for every individual. This is why everyone needs to participate in the decisions that are made. It is also important to take steps to resolve any communication problem and prevent potential communication difficulties. It is normal to have conflict in close relationships. Living and/or working closely together will occasionally give rise to misunderstandings. Every individual on the team has a unique personality, history, tastes, lifestyle, and needs. These differences frequently result in conflict. Accepting conflict as a part of team life will help us deal with it better. Conflict in and of itself is not destructive. How we manage conflict determines how destructive it is. It is a fact that teams that manage conflict well sometimes grow closer.

Teams under severe stress generally become less tolerant. The ability to handle intense internal and external stress can be significantly compromised. With internal stress, there is a greater likelihood of developing problems like fatigue, anxiety, unresolved inner conflict, physical illness, and hormonal changes. Team employees should avoid dealing with serious conflict when they are under a lot of stress.

Arguments and disputes can occur on any team. However, constant, long-lasting disputes and friction between team members is damaging to the team. Resolving disputes in the right way can strengthen team spirit and boost team loyalty.

A team that engages in productive conflict by listening to the opinions and ideas of the other members will remain supportive of the team decisions and implement them because of their trust and because they know that everyone's input was taken into consideration.

Communication Barriers And Methods That Facilitate Communication

The quality of the communication between team members is critical. The Team Coach fosters a safe setting so that team members can work through issues in a healthy way. In order to maintain this environment, both the Team Coach and the team members must be careful not to create barriers to communication.

The following information on four barriers to communication is based on research conducted by John Gottman. Gottman describes these four behaviors as the four horsemen of the apocalypse. When you hear the horsemen approaching, communication problems are bearing down upon you.

- Blame/Criticism
- Defensiveness
- Stonewalling
- Contempt

Communication Barriers	
Blame/Criticism	Targeting the person rather than the behavior. "You are not thinking right." "You have always been lazy anyway." The message is that a person is inadequate, stupid, or incorrect. Fear of being the target of negative judgment or scolding will result in the person cutting off communication. People generally perceive judgment or criticism as truth (I am bad), and they respond by starting to defend themselves (as if they are perfect).

Methods That Facilitate Communication	
Blame/Criticism	Can you express this without laying blame? Specify the behavior you don't like without targeting the person who did it. Use a soft entry. Convert your criticisms into requests. Use language that includes the words "I feel" and "I want."

Communication Barriers	
Defensiveness	Attitudes that are judgmental, controlling, strategic, indifferent, rigid, and communicate superiority. Defensiveness is an attempt to defend oneself from perceived attack. It includes righteous indignation, or counterattack, an impulse to immediately refute whatever might be coming.

Methods That Facilitate Communication	
Defensiveness	Listening without getting defensive is a hard skill to master. Focus on active listening when team members are not really hearing each other. "Gary, I hear you saying xyz" is an example. Control the intensity and take a break if necessary. "I'm trying to listen, but I am taking this personally. Can we take a 10-minute break? Your perspective is important to me, and I want to be sure I understand you."

Communication Barriers	
Stonewalling	This includes cutting off communication, the silent treatment, refusing to build relationships and not responding. In other words, people wall themselves in. It may be considered a natural defense mechanism for a person who experiences blame, defensiveness, and belittling to leave the relationship at some point and to build walls to protect themselves. It may be natural, but this is unfortunately no comfort to others. In a normal relationship, the parties give signs to indicate that they are listening to and understanding each other. A person who builds a wall gives no reaction. When they leave their environment, they leave the team as well.
Methods That Facilitate Communication	
Stonewalling	If one member is quiet, as the Team Coach, you can ask for permission to speak as their double. "Anna, I see that you aren't saying anything, and I have an idea what you are thinking. Would it be okay with you if I share this and you can say whether or not I am right?" "Gary, the reason we are doing this is to make sure Anna's opinion is heard. I am only saying this out loud. I am not defending an idea." After you have shared this, give Anna a chance to speak for herself as soon as possible. Talk about the fears that a person has about what will happen if they speak. Encourage dialogue by considering the other side of the dispute.

Communication Barriers	
Contempt	Contempt is the most destructive negative behavior in relationships. It is poisonous because it conveys disgust and superiority. Contemptuous behaviors include insinuation, belittling, mocking, name-calling, and hostile humor. Body language can include eye-rolling and sneering. It is virtually impossible to resolve a problem when the other person is getting the message that you are disgusted with them or you are condescending.

Methods That Facilitate Communication	
Contempt	Describe your own feelings and needs about any given issue. Try to avoid using "you" statements. Use sentences that begin with "I feel, I want ..." The more positive you feel, the less likely you'll feel or express contempt. Remind yourself of positive qualities and express appreciation, gratitude, affection, and respect. End a conversation with a statement of appreciation.

It is very normal to see these types of interaction between team members. Many people display these behaviors on occasion. The important thing is to recognize these types of communication barriers among team members and then to emphasize the importance of eliminating them while describing a more desirable form of communication to replace them. It is the Team Coach's responsibility to initiate this process.

obstacles

Communication Barriers On The Team And Methods That Facilitate Communication

Purpose: Facilitating communication between team members and raising awareness about communication barriers.

Duration: 50 minutes.

Materials: Sticky notepads, pens, and whiteboard.

After telling the participants about Gottman's four horsemen of the apocalypse, set up boards for these behaviors in the four corners of the classroom. Sticky notepads are passed out to the participants, who are asked to write down the words or phrases most often used when these behaviors occur and then to put them on the appropriate board. (10 minutes)

Then the phrases used most frequently on the boards will be selected to identify the obstructive language used by the team. Discuss what team members feel when this language is used. (15 minutes)

The second phase consists of providing information about methods that facilitate communication. The participants are then asked to write down words/phrases to replace the language they used to use that was a barrier to communication. They will tear up the old ones and post the new ones on the boards. (10 minutes) The phrases that occur most frequently on the boards will be selected to identify the healthy language the team will use in the future. Discuss what team members feel when this language is used. (15 minutes)

Nonviolent Communication

Marshall B. Rosenberg was the first person to define *Nonviolent Communication*. As Rosenberg describes in his book, nonviolent communication is based on language and communication skills that reinforce our ability to behave humanely even under challenging conditions. Nonviolent communication serves as a guide for people to develop a new framework of talking with and listening to others. When words are transformed from instinctive reactions to extremely aware responses, this minimizes resistance, extreme reactions, and the tendency to be defensive.

The first component of nonviolent communication is being able to distinguish between observation and assessment. If this distinction is not made, the listener will feel criticized and be resistant to receiving the message. Generalizations can hurt communication, so observations should be directed at a specific time and context. For example, instead of saying "X is a terrible football player," say "X has not been able to score in twenty matches."

Learning to separate an observation from a judgment is key, and raises the likelihood that the person listening will be more willing to hear our feelings and needs.

The second component required for a person to express themselves is emotion. The better we are at clearly expressing our emotions, the better our communication will flow and the easier it will be to resolve disputes. Identify, name and connect with your feelings. Describe how you feel (an emotion or sensation rather than a thought). "I feel disappointed" describes your experience, while "I don't feel that you trust me" is an interpretation of how the other person may be feeling.

The third component is an awareness of the needs behind the emotions. What others say or do can evoke a range of emotions in a person, but they are not actually the reason for the emotions. Connecting with and expressing the need behind the emotions creates space for the need to be met in several different ways. Focus on the need, not the action. Whenever we include a person, location, action, time, or object in our expression, we are describing a strategy rather than a need. "I need to be able to voice my own opinion" instead of "John needs to stop speaking for me in meetings."

The fourth component is what individuals can ask of each other to enrich their lives. Avoid ambiguous, abstract, and confusing language. Requests are different from demands. Requests are made in the present and are doable, concrete, and specific. Good requests focus on expressing what *is* wanted and not on what is *not* wanted. "Would you be willing to lower your voice or talk later?" rather than what we want them to stop doing ("Don't yell at me.") or how we want them to be ("Treat me with respect.").

We can only empathize with someone when we focus on hearing what the person we are interacting with actually means and feels when they are talking. Empathy is respectfully understanding the lives of others. What we usually do instead of empathizing is give advice, try to comfort them, or explain our situation. Empathy means allowing the other person to express themselves.

Empathy is an effective listening technique. But it doesn't always lead us to a solution. Sometimes, it is impossible to ignore certain facts that go beyond feelings and be more objective. When we are listening and trying to understand a teammate who claims to have a brilliant idea, being objective can help us see that the idea is actually completely unrealistic. Expressing oneself clearly is just as critical as good listening. Using terms that our teammates do not know and highlighting political opinions, upbringing, culture, and age differences would be wrong.

Remember that blaming and punishing others are outward signs of anger. A person who wants to express their anger must absolve the other person from any responsibility for his/her anger. Instead, the focus should be on the person's own emotions and needs. If needs are expressed instead of blaming or judging others, it is more likely that these needs will be met.

Some Methods That Facilitate Communication

As a Team Coach, you can use the following techniques for eliminating communication styles that create barriers between team members.

1. When communication barriers occur, give them a name, and share information about their negative effects and how they hurt the team. In other words, raise awareness on the team.
2. Create a shared password or gesture for these communication barriers on the team. This is an especially important part of the team agreement. The password or gesture that you create is meant to serve as an indicator, not to show that team members are guilty. Everyone does not have to agree that the communication in question is a toxic barrier. The important thing is simply that the team becomes aware of toxic behavior.
3. Do not allow too many communication infractions. If necessary, end the meeting or take a break.

Feedback Between Team Members

Daughter, I am telling you, so that my daughter-in-law will understand.—Turkish Proverb

This is one of the most well-known sayings in my beautiful country, but it is at the top of the list of dangerous communication styles that a leader must avoid. Those who have personal experience with this know only too well that in this approach the person who commits the act pays no heed to what is said, but the one who does what is necessary and successfully completes his work is bombarded with negativity and demoralized.

Another aspect of this approach is that indirect communication between team members is like blowing up the foundation of the relationship and opens the door to the toxic communication styles referred to as the four horsemen of the apocalypse: aggression, building walls, defensiveness, and contempt. In his book entitled *Blink*, Malcolm Gladwell, the renowned author who for years ranked above heads of state on the list of people who had the greatest impact on the American public, proved that frequent use of these communication styles whenever there is a difference of opinion or dispute in interpersonal relationships is the most important cause of relationship failure or difficulty.

Therefore, ensuring that the feedback/feedforward and communication on our teams, whether that is one-on-one or teamwide, occurs without falling into the traps I have described above is critical if we want the synergy that we have or will create on the team to be sustainable and long-lasting.

Feedback is different from defensiveness as a response to a certain behavior or action. Giving feedback is an important part of being a manager or a coach. This give-and-take continues throughout the process of identifying important issues during the coaching process, developing action plans, and evaluating the results.

Try to practice the following when giving feedback, regardless of whether it is positive or negative.

Focus on the behavior, not who the person is. Feedback is not passing judgment but describing behavior. You should be explaining to the team member the impact of their behavior. Avoid passing judgment or characterizing them with adjectives. Do not use the words "good" or "bad." Judgmental language will make the person defensive or prevent them from hearing you. Let the other person form their own conclusion about the effects of their behavior on you.

> For example: Instead of saying, "You are disrespectful and inconsiderate," try saying "I have seen you interrupt Mike in each of the last three meetings we had."
>
> Instead of saying, "You are arrogant," say, "You said that my idea was worthless."
>
> Instead of saying, "You are so polite," say "You smiled at me and looked me in the eye."

Be specific. Avoid generalizations. For example, instead of saying, "You did a good job," you can say, "The things you used in your presentation were amazingly effective at communicating your message to the audience."

Be sincere. Make it clear that your aim is to help the person improve.

Be realistic. Focus on situations that the person can actually control. Share how the behavior affected you and the effect that you observed on others. For example, "This made me withdraw from the conversation, but this made me feel comfortable on the team."

Give your feedback in a timely manner and generally during the coaching time. Feedback that is given frequently and immediately after the incident is more effective than infrequent feedback.

Feedback is not a way to communicate what you want. If you want something, say it without beating around the bush. Do not engage in passive-aggressive behavior. For example, instead of saying, "You are delaying my project," say, "I am waiting for you to approve my project."

Do not give advice, but information. The purpose of feedback is for team members to understand and accept how their behavior affects others, not to change the behavior of the team member.

Feedback should always be given with good intentions. Effective feedback is actually like a gift that you give to the team, and gifts should meet the needs of the recipient. Remember that feedback is not finding the team's mistakes and "fixing" them!

Feedforward Between Team Members

Feedforward is recognized as being just as important as feedback in effective coaching. Feedback focuses on the past. Profiles created in connection with what has happened or transpired provide the team with information for the purposes of evaluation. Team members also want information about what will be done now and in the future. Sharing ideas about what team members want, what they want to do, and possible changes they will need in the future is also important to the team. This is the purpose of the feedforward process.

Marshall Goldsmith recommends a simple method to achieve this objective.

1. Have the team members choose a behavior that they have agreed to change, will embrace, and which will make a positive contribution.
2. Have the members of the team define this selected behavior. For example, "We will be more effective listeners."
3. Do not allow feedback from the past, but keep them focused on the future, and make a list of their ideas about the future.
4. Do not allow comments about opinions. Every member of the team should be able to convey their recommendations, possibilities, and choices without being judged. Do not block criticism, but show your support for appreciating and recognizing others. "Now that is a good idea!" would be an example.
5. Ask the members of the team what changes they want.
6. Clarify which options the team will use to change and improve.
7. Turn these choices into goals and have the team monitor their progress.
8. Repeat this process at regular intervals.

Receiving Feedback/Feedforward

It is also particularly important that team members be open to receiving feedback/feedforward from each other. You simply must be open to feedback about your performance. Coaches and team members who ask for feedback and actually consider it will learn more about how effective their leadership style is and will build trust with their team.

Here are some steps to improving your ability to receive feedback:

- Do not put the team on the defensive when asking for transparency. Instead of saying, "What do you mean when you say that I responded negatively to the idea you put forward?" you can say, "Can you give me an example?"
- Ask for specific information. For example, "What did I say that gave you the idea that I was uninterested in your suggestion?" Another example would be, "How have my recommendations been beneficial?"
- Be open to both negative and positive feedback.
- Encourage the team to avoid the use of emotionally charged language.
- Do not be defensive. Only justify your actions when asked to do so. When you receive more feedback/feedforward than you can effectively implement, let the team know this.
- Whether it is positive or negative, always thank the team for providing feedback. Your gratitude will reinforce the team's confidence in you and your role-modeling behavior. We know in coaching that the emotional context of any conversation impacts/generates certain outcomes. We are always in some emotion when we speak or listen. So ask the team what emotions would support both giving and receiving feedback. If someone does not feel safe, receiving feedback automatically creates distrust or resistance.

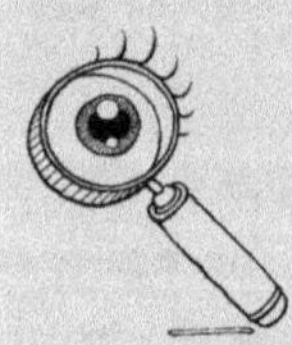

Hint

Team Coach Rules for Feedback/Feedforward:

- Let the team members talk first.
- Increase the amount of positive feedback and feedforward.
- Be straightforward with what you have to say.
- Focus on a few key points. Do not push too much.
- Avoid personal feedback/feedforward with the whole team. Do this behind closed doors.
- Give your feedback/feedforward to the team, not to individuals.
- Balance the feedback/feedforward: strengths versus areas of improvement.
- Be bold. There may be opportunities in areas of improvement.
- Be transparent and honest.
- Trust and be trustworthy.
- Take timely action. Do not put things off.
- Do not be a mediator.
- Trust the feedback/feedforward and believe in its effectiveness.
- Give praise.
- Temper your anger: If feedback/feedforward is given when angry, the focus is on the anger.
- Be an example.
- Act like you are open to feedback/feedforward and request it.

but
and

ACTIVITY

Giving and Receiving Feedback

Purpose: To raise team awareness of the importance of improving their observational skills and giving good feedback.

Duration: 10 minutes per person.

Materials: Paper and pens. Work in groups of three.

For three minutes, A will give B feedback about areas of improvement he/she has observed in B, and how these make A feel. C will observe and take notes about how B responds and B's body language.

Two minutes will be spent sharing observations.

Then, for three minutes A will give feedback to B about strengths he/she has observed and how these make A feel. C will observe and take notes about how B responds to what he/she hears and B's body language.

Two minutes will be spent sharing observations.

Then they switch the roles: For three minutes, B will give C feedback about areas of improvement he/she has observed in C, and how these make B feel. A will observe and take notes about how C responds and C's body language.

Two minutes will be spent sharing observations.

Then, for three minutes B will give feedback to C about strengths they have observed and how these make B feel. A will observe and take notes about how C responds to what he/she hears and C's body language.

Two minutes will be spent sharing observations.

In the final round, for three minutes, C will give A feedback about areas of improvement he/she has observed in A, and how these make C feel. B will observe and take notes about how A responds and A's body language.

Two minutes will be spent sharing observations.

Then, for three minutes C will give feedback to A about strengths they have observed and how these make C feel. B will observe and take notes about how A responds to what he/she hears and A's body language.

Conflict Between Team Members

A good team knows exactly how to deal with conflict and agrees to handle it. Conflicts arising from stress and disagreements are inevitable, and there are both positives and negatives to this kind of stress. An advantage of conflict is that it boosts energy and concentration levels. The disadvantages include resistance and defensiveness.

Productive conflict is actually required for all healthy relationships to grow. It is just as true for the workplace as it is for marriage, raising children, and friendship.

Whether it is a simple matter or a critical decision, whether it is between two people or a group, conflict is part of life. Unfortunately, many people make dealing with conflict difficult for themselves because of their "personal" outlook on the issues. If conflict increases team participation and efforts to resolve the problem, then it can be characterized as positive. However, conflict is harmful if it directs the team's energy to unimportant and trivial matters, has a negative impact on the team and/or individuals, or results in polarization.

Effective teams discuss problems and quickly resolve issues completely.

However, conflict is generally regarded as taboo. Lots of people actually spend valuable time and energy avoiding conflict. It is important to distinguish between productive conflicts and destructive arguments or political maneuvering between individuals. If the conflict is limited to concepts and ideas and if malicious attacks focused on people are avoided, it is productive and beneficial. A productive conflict will quickly bring the team to the best resolution. Effective teams discuss problems and quickly resolve them. When the argument is over, they are enthusiastic and willing to take on the next problem as they have not taken offense or lost confidence.

Teams that avoid conflict do this without hurting each other's feelings, but in the end, they cannot prevent dangerous tensions from occurring. When team members do not have transparent debates, they can quickly turn into personal attacks and be hurtful.

A healthy conflict boosts productivity because it prevents time from being wasted. Although discussions may appear to be a waste of time, actually every unresolved issue has been revisited again and again, which makes the team feel like a failure.

Teams that fear conflict

- Have boring meetings.
- Create an atmosphere conducive to personal attacks and behind-the-scenes maneuvering.
- Ignore controversial issues that are critical to the team's success.
- Fail to take into account the views of all the team members.
- Waste time and energy taking positions.
- Lay the foundation for backbiting.

Teams that engage in conflict

- Have lively and interesting meetings.
- Hear and utilize the ideas of all the team members.
- Quickly resolve real problems.
- Ensure that behind-the-scenes maneuvering is reduced to a minimum.
- Put critical issues on the table for discussion.

The reasons for conflict in teamwork may be scarcity of resources, overlapping duties or failure to perform duties, poor communication, personal differences, power struggles, or unattainable goals. Whatever the reason, effective teams are those that can address these issues.

The renowned philosopher Martin Buber talks about the importance of not closing ourselves off to the other person when debating sensitive matters, and staying in control of ourselves without ignoring their needs. During conflict, we generally either forgo our own needs or become hostile in an attempt to make people agree with us. The question that Buber asks at this point is how you can remain open to hearing about other people's needs without compromising yourself when debating sensitive matters.

Clinical psychologist David Schnarch says that conflict in close relationships is good because it nurtures and grows the relationship. When a discussion of sensitive issues ceases to be a verbal duel and becomes a place where the parties understand each other and cooperate, relationships can move to another level.

Practical Methods For The Team Coach: Handling Conflict

Method 1: Occasionally assign team members who avoid conflict the task of "conflict mining." The purpose here is to bring to light misunderstandings that have been buried by the team. The team should be encouraged to be resolute in terms of remaining neutral by continuing the conflict until the issues in question are resolved. The team might consider giving this responsibility to one of the members during a specific meeting or discussion.

Method 2: If a creative dispute gets out of hand or gets deadlocked, the members begin unproductive arguing. Immediately intervene and refocus them on the team goal. The question you should ask is "What do you want to achieve?"

Method 3: Recognizing the moment when the people participating in the discussion feel uncomfortable with the level of dispute and immediately intervening to remind them that what they are doing is really important. This is a vital form of support the Team Coach adds. It is critical that this tension be mitigated, and that support and encouragement be provided. When the discussion is over, the Team Coach should remind everyone that the conflict they engaged in was helpful to the team and that they should not avoid it in the future

Method 4: Disputes arising from personal or mutual power struggles can be much more destructive than creative disputes.

If, as the Team Coach, you do not act skillfully and resolutely to openly address disputes, this will end up being one of the biggest obstacles to the team making progress. If you avoid the issue because you are worried someone's feelings will be hurt, the team will have trouble transitioning to the next phase. Unresolved disputes will get even worse and eventually make it impossible for the team to do anything.

Method 5: Situation assessment:

- Is it a creative and constructive dispute?
- Is any inequality involved?
- Is there a lack of appreciation?
- Are there conflicting personality types?
- Is it due to differing perspectives?
- Is incompetence or negligence involved?

These are the types of questions that you need to ask yourself—or if necessary, the team—to understand the underlying problem in the dispute.

Method 6: If the team conflicts are always between the same people, sometimes these people need to swap roles and be asked to continue the discussion in the other person's shoes. As the Team Coach, it is critical that you help the team members gain awareness of how their actions affect the team. This will sometimes be a positive contribution, other times a negative one.

Method 7: Recognizing team communication approaches that create barriers and giving them a symbol so that the members of the team can focus their attention on this will raise awareness.

The Team Coach is responsible for putting a stop to or preventing actions that create a feeling of guilt, shift blame to others, are rude or irritable, cut off communication, take the path of least resistance, blow disputes out of proportion, are belittling or avoid responsibility. As a Team Coach, you must not avoid conflicts between team members. It is important to recognize your instinctive desire to protect the members of the team and accept the fact that preventing conflict only escalates the tension. It is also essential that the Team Coach be a role model in conflict.

SCAPEGOAT
JOE

ACTIVITY

Difficult Team Member

Purpose: To raise awareness on the team about conflict and conflict management.

Duration: 15 minutes.

Materials: Paper with a text written on it, note paper and pens.

Divide the team into smaller groups of 4–6 people. Give the following text to each group on a piece of paper:

Occasionally, each of us becomes the "difficult" team member. We might be stressed out, tired, or confused. We do not contribute as much as we normally would.

Imagine a team member with every negative trait. What would that look like? What kinds of traits would result in being excluded from the group?

Every group/team should think about and discuss this question for five minutes. Make sure the entire team is included in the discussion by using the following questions:

- Which traits are harmful?
- Have you ever experienced any of these traits? Which one? What can be done about this?
- How did this activity help you be more productive teammates?
- What traits should a productive teammate have?
- What is your personal responsibility toward the team?

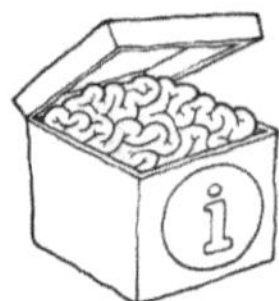

SIDEBAR

Alliance-Building for Effective Teams

Reid Hoffman, Ben Casnocha, and Chris Yeh are three people with extensive entrepreneurial experience. Together they wrote a book entitled *The Alliance: Managing Talent in the Networked Age,* which brings a new perspective to employer-employee relationships.

The paradigm shift that has occurred in the workplace in recent years has damaged the trust between employers and employees. As a result, the workplace looks more and more like a place where everyone suffers.

The world is changing both technologically and philosophically. With the rise of capitalism, managers began setting only short-term goals to raise share values. Therefore, the employer-employee relationship turned into an artificial relationship built on a system of exchange with strict rules and a serious lack of trust. The false notion that the employer has the same goal as the employee is unraveling. Even though the employer focuses on issues like "talent management," "team," and "family," employees will quickly find themselves separated from the work environment or the team that they viewed as "family" if the company's short-term objectives are not met. Employees who work under this implied threat cannot feel any "loyalty" to this system. No employee wants to invest in a long-term relationship, because they are worried about being shown the door.

Because no one wants to make this investment, everyone suffers, even the companies. A job without loyalty is a job without reliable long-term plans. It is impossible to invest in the future without a long-term plan. Unless companies can see the opportunities and technologies of the future, they are already in the process of going bust.

It is impossible to bring back the company dynamics that existed in the past, so a new kind of loyalty has to be fostered. By recognizing economic truths, the bond of loyalty between companies and employees can be reestablished. This new model is the alliance model. There is even a book on the topic by the same name. This business model is built on mutual trust, reciprocal investment, and profit sharing. As companies take an approach that can be summarized as "You bring value to our business, and we will share that value with you," employees are saying, "You help me grow and become prosperous, and I will help the company grow and become prosperous." Tour of duty is a distinctive part of this business model. Just like soldiers in the military, employees who complete a specific task assigned to them can stay at the same company if they wish and choose to take on new challenges. In the book, tours of duty are separated into three types.

- Rotational: Entry-level, the most common tour.
- Transformational: A more personal and more intense tour. The employee strives to improve both their own career and the company's future.
- Foundational: This includes CEOs and senior executives.

Tour of duty allows companies to retain their most talented employees, and the employees can create their own "personal brands." This is how reciprocal trust is created. Improved conditions in the workplace may be the beginning of tremendous social progress. The small changes that we make today may pave the way for huge transformation in the future.

Appreciation Between Team Members

One of the most effective ways to motivate both individuals and teams is to show appreciation. According to the latest research on positive psychology and power-based leadership, teams that focus on what is going right instead of problems and weaknesses actually grow stronger.

Marshall Rosenberg says there is a huge need for real appreciation in the workplace, and not just empty praise given to score points. When a manager heaps empty praise on his employees, they may begin working harder, but this will be short-lived. When the employees realize that this praise is actually a form of manipulation and exploitation, their productivity will fall. People can sense it when praise is used as a means to an end and is not heartfelt. In this situation, the recognition or appreciation is meaningless.

In sincere communication, the only purpose of appreciation is to congratulate someone for doing a good job. It is not about manipulation or getting something in return. It is also true that many people do not graciously accept appreciation. They weigh whether or not they are worthy of the appreciation and worry that something is expected in return. When appreciation is shown to someone, they should accept the fact that they have the power to make other people's lives better. This prevents it from going to their head or them developing an attitude of false humility. Appreciation should be accepted by celebrating with the person who expresses their thanks without succumbing to false humility or feeling superior.

Appreciation

Purpose: To help the team make a habit of expressing appreciation and experiencing the resulting positive atmosphere together.

Duration: 15 minutes.

Materials: Paper and pens.

Everyone treats the exercise like a cocktail party and walks around asking each other the following three questions.

- What do you appreciate most about yourself?
- What do you appreciate most about the person in front of you?
- What team trait do you appreciate the most?

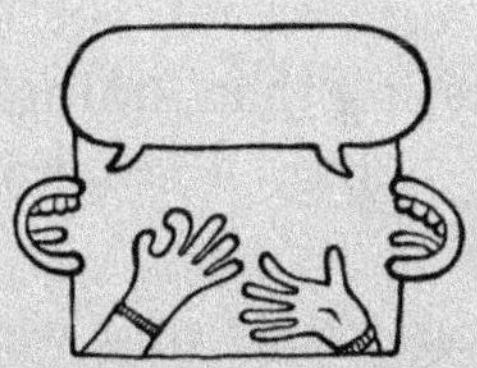

Discussion Time

What kind of atmosphere was created by expressing appreciation? What did you feel? How did it change the atmosphere? What did you observe?

Nonverbal Communication: Using Body Language

There are two aspects of communication: verbal and nonverbal communication. Most studies address the issue of verbal communication, but science has shown that nonverbal communication is actually much more powerful. In particular, we can express emotions much more effectively and indirectly through nonverbal communication. It is easier to express thoughts with verbal communication and emotions through nonverbal communication. Understanding what emotions mean and experiencing their impact in a healthy way is also important.

We access the unique resources we possess by experiencing emotions instead of talking about them. What would it be like to start your day with the following question rather than with a seemingly endless to-do list? "How do I want to feel at the end of the day?" This question could be immediately followed by "What do I need in order to experience this feeling?" Of course, no one is suggesting that "doing" be neglected in order to remain in a place of "being." Rather, it is letting "our being" affect "our doing."

There are six basic emotions that we experience. These are expressed in the involuntary movements of the 47 muscles in the face. They can be summarized as anger, fear, surprise, sadness, happiness, and disgust.

The emotion occurs and matures in 1–5 seconds. It is reflected in our expression between 2–4 seconds, first in the voice, then in the facial expression and body posture. In other words, first emotions are felt, and then they manifest physically.

And there is always a constant dynamic interaction between discourse, body, and emotions, meaning that any one can influence another. When we shift our body, our emotion can change. When we say something, it can generate emotions. When we feel a certain way, our body and language reflect that emotion. They are always interacting and impacting each other. When we become aware of this dynamic, we gain the capacity to make conscious shifts in any part of these three important domains: Discourse, Emotions, and Body.

The body and emotions are being interpreted before language begins. The question is, are we aware of how much we transmit to others nonverbally and are we observant of how much we "read" another person before they speak?

When words and their physical reflection are in harmony, actions that produce results are manifested, which ensures transparency on the team. Relationships are also built on a truer foundation.

If team members can build their relationships with physical presence and become skilled at reading body language, they will have accessed an important resource toward achieving their goals. It is also important for the Team Coach to be skilled at understanding their own physical expression of emotion but also provide feedback to the group in light of his/her own intuitions and to observe the harmony between language-emotion-body among the team members.

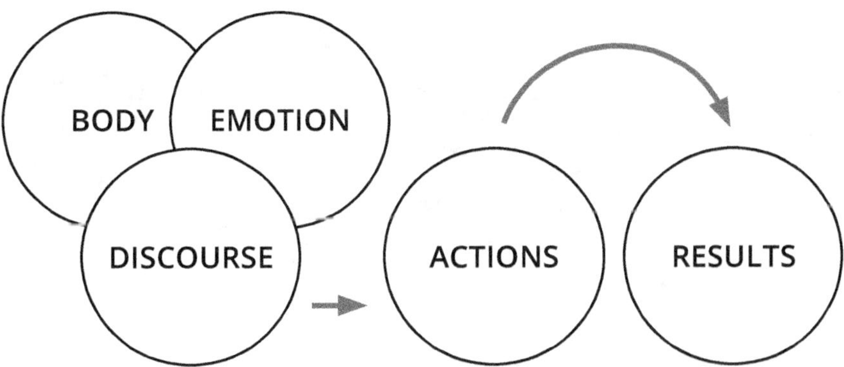

ACTIVITY

How Body Language Affects Expression And Emotion

Purpose: To observe different physical reactions and create awareness of the fact that the body is a source of information.

Duration: 15 minutes.

Materials: Different types of music and a spacious area.

This is a physical exercise with music that the entire group does. The purpose is to try different movements and understand the effects.

Participants will experiment with physical activity like a military march or choreographed dance, such as folk dances, and with free dance.

The group will discuss what emotions they experience with different types of music and physical movements.

SIDEBAR

Effective Teamwork Methods

Problems in the workplace are on the rise. Employee productivity is declining due to the various problems experienced in the workplace. Managers are struggling to control their employees, while more and more people hate their job.

There are three main rules that must be followed on a team facing these types of problems:

1. Identify the problem with the highest priority.

The team must identify which of the problems it faces is having the most negative effect and list the facts surrounding this problem. The impact of this negative situation needs to be analyzed. They must try to figure out what are the real underlying causes and create an environment that sheds light on the matter.

2. Identify the method you will use to resolve the problem.

The team must analyze the ways in which it has tried to resolve the problem in the past, and it must abandon these approaches if they were not effective.

3. Research new feasible solutions to replace those that don't work

Find and implement a surprising method that is out of the ordinary. If this solution doesn't work, keep looking. Motivate the team to create an alternative if another solution doesn't work. The tactics of "reverse psychology" may be helpful. If there is a member of the team who is constantly critical and does not change in spite of you calling it to their attention multiple times, they will look at this matter differently if you constantly ask them for criticism.

Generally, when people are trying to change the person they are dealing with, it is clear that they are hung up on a solution and that they cannot find a way out. Everything changes when we look at events from a fresh perspective and get rid of unproductive methods.

The traits of teams that perform well

In order to get the desired benefit from a team, its effectiveness must be boosted. The following are necessary to achieve a boost in team productivity:

- Specify the roles and responsibilities of team members.
- Provide team members with the training they need to hone their skills.
- Ensure optimal utilization of the resources on the team.
- Set clear performance targets that members can agree on.
- Establish team culture and effective leadership.
- Create rituals for appreciation and recognition between team members.

ACTIVITY

Building Our Tower

Purpose: To experience how a team functions with limited time and fluctuating conditions.

Duration: 25 minutes.

Materials: Tape measure or ruler, 50 index cards for each group, adhesive tape for each group, and a small prize for the group that wins.

In this activity, the team members build a tower from the cards that are passed out.

Divide the team into groups of 3–5 people. Give each group 25 cards and adhesive tape. Tell them to build the largest structure possible in ten minutes. After they are finished, the structure will be measured with a ruler and the teams will be told to tear down the structures. Then, you will announce that adhesive tape is banned because it is a health hazard and give 25 more cards to each team. Again, they will be asked to build as big a structure as possible in five minutes. When the time is up, the structures will be measured, and the biggest will be announced the winner. The winning group will be given a prize.

Questions:

- How did you decide on the structure you would build?
- How did you feel when adhesive tape was banned?
- What kind of methods did you use to achieve success in phase two?
- What did this game teach you about your career?

Team Coaching Skills: Creating Common Team Goals

Setting Goals on a Team

We were starting a workshop with the executive committee of a family company that was talking about its five-year goal of being in the top ten in their sector, if not number one. The team was sincere and focused on results. It consisted of two brothers, their sister and father as well as two professional high-level executives who had just joined the company, and another professional executive who had been with the company for three years.

At the beginning of the workshop, I asked them to write down their company goal for the next year without talking to each other and to put it in a sealed envelope in a glass jar I had brought with me. Their surprise was evident from their facial expressions, but they quickly recovered and wrote the goal on the paper in front of them, sealed it in the envelope, and put it in the jar.

Fifteen minutes later, the only way to describe the room was stunned silence. The main reason for this consternation was that there were seven completely unrelated goals in these envelopes, though each was especially important and even critical for the company to progress. The result was also very surprising to me, but in fact this is a common problem that teams face: setting a common goal, holding each other accountable in a healthy way while moving toward this goal and only arguing with others about the issue at hand.

How do you set a shared goal for your team and keep it in focus?

Daydreaming is generally considered a waste of time, but scientific studies have shown that imagination is an inseparable part of the creative process.

 *Logic will get you from A to B. Imagination will take you everywhere.* —Albert Einstein

The level of civilization and prosperity that humanity has now achieved is the result of people and communities following their dreams and goals.

Without a vision and goals, we are doomed to wander aimlessly, like a ship without a destination. Dreaming makes it possible to discover ideas and to imagine new situations.

Recent scientific studies have begun to find proof that this is true. Tests conducted as part of research at the University of California–Santa Barbara have demonstrated that people who use their imagination are 41% more creative in their thinking compared to other people.

 *I dream of painting and then I paint my dream.* —Van Gogh

Dreaming is critical to motivation and motivation to success. A clear and concrete dream or goal is what facilitates action and moves us to act, motivates us, and excites us. Productivity is proportionally related to excitement. Faith takes a person where they want to be and begins to provide results immediately.

Psychologist E. Paul Torrance studied IQ tests, academic achievement, and other indicators of success for a group of people from elementary school to the age of 30. The conclusion reached by this long-term study was that grades and similar measures were insignificant factors in whether or not a person would be successful in life. The most important determinative factor was what kind of life the children envisioned for themselves as adults.

This is why the Team Coach must understand the personal dreams of the team members and support the team's shared dream. When a team has low performance, one of the most common reasons is problems with team objectives. Factors that have a negative effect on team performance include failure to focus on goals, politicization of goals, and a team that is lax about its goals or about making personal goals a priority. When the goals are clearly specified, it helps the team members make decisions about which issues to concentrate the majority of their time on and which issues the Team Coach needs to be more involved with.

Specific performance targets will improve team productivity. These goals must be clear, comprehensible, easily observable, and measurable. It is important to have the team involved when setting these goals.

Good goals are those chosen with expertise. Here are some characteristics of good goals:

- They should be specific. They should preclude assumptions and should be focused.
- They should be measurable. They should facilitate observation of progress.
- They should be attainable. Ambitious goals that are also realistic provide a challenge.
- There should be a way to reward its achievement, because people like to do things that will be rewarded.
- It should have time parameters.
- It should be framed in positive language. Use "What we want" instead of "What we don't want."

S	M	A	R	T
Specific	Measurable	Achievable	Relevant	Time-Bound

A team that does not focus on results

- Cannot make headway or improve.
- Very rarely overtakes the competition.
- Will lose people focused on success.
- Will encourage team members to focus on their own careers and individual goals.
- Will be easily distracted.

A team that focuses on a shared goal

- Will retain people focused on success.
- Will minimize individualistic behavior.
- Will be delighted with success and upset about failure.
- Will benefit from individuals that use their own goals and interests to help the team.
- Will avoid distractions.

The Team Coach must be sure that team goals are understood by the team. This helps avoid the following common problems:

- Goal uncertainty: This refers to goals that have not been clearly stated.
- Goal conflict: The differences between the goals of the team members, the team leader, the clients, and the company.
- Goal-loading: Unrealistic goals are morale-busters for the team and damage members' self-confidence.
- Goal complexity: Complex goals that cannot be measured can never be satisfying.

The team's job is to create and implement alternatives that will resolve the various problems that are a threat to the achievement of its strategic objectives and that prevent the organization from functioning properly.

You as a team coach or a leader need to facilitate for clearly defined "conditions of satisfaction" and "how you are going to celebrate the success" in advance to establish an emotional connection to the goals.

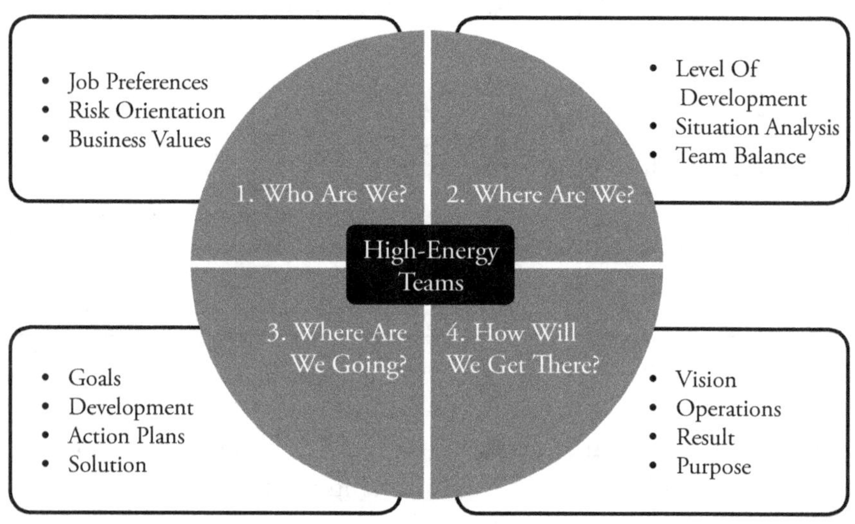

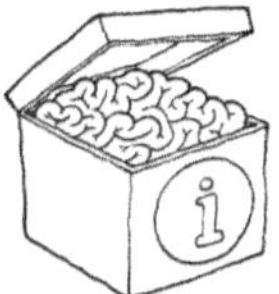

SIDEBAR

Rowing Teams

In his book *Blue Jean Executive* (*Kot Pantolonlu Yönetici*), Murat Toktamışoğlu gives an interesting description of rowing teams.

There are two functions on a rowing team: the scullers and the coxswain. The scullers have their backs to the direction they are moving. The athletes do not communicate with each other. They row by quickly looking at someone whose face is turned toward them. The scullers cannot see the destination, but they know where it is. Everyone is putting out maximum effort and their performance is based on harmony and balance, keeping the same tempo, as they move toward the objective. A team that is facing backward and moving toward a common goal without speaking while complementing each other and creating synergy is a tremendous display of resolve. This is what you call teamwork.

The person who directs the team is the coxswain, who sits in the back of the boat. The coxswain does not row, but that person is the leader on the team's journey. The leader's job is to sustain and standardize the course and rhythm. The leader is also a member of the team, and an especially important one. One wrong move or break in the rhythm can destroy everything, causing a course deviation. The goal is in their hearts and they think of nothing else. They move toward the goal thanks to the coxswain's direction and the tempo he or she sets. Leaders in organizations must also be able to direct employees toward the goal while preserving harmony and balance.

ACTIVITY

Magic Wand

Purpose: To experience goal clarification and the power of setting goals together as a team and to use the wisdom of the body.

Duration: 20 minutes.

Materials: Paper and pens.

The participants are divided into groups of five. Each participant is given three minutes. The trainers ask the participants to imagine that they hold a magic wand in their hands and tell them: "If you could only change one thing with the magic wand so that the team would achieve its goals, what would it be?" The coach asks the participants to find a physical gesture that will function as the magic wand. Then, everyone uses their own gestures to indicate what they want for the team one year from now.

Discussion Time

After the individual sharing, note which dreams the team shares. Discuss the importance of using your imagination to dream. Discuss the mechanisms that the participants use in their daily lives as a way to engage their imagination.

Making Choices in the Pursuit of Team Objectives

Conscious choices are those made by individuals in control, but reactions are automatic, unconscious, and uncontrolled. Unconscious decisions become a person's habits.

The most important decision is the decision a person makes about their own attitude. This is a critical point that deserves reflection:

Only you choose how you want to look at things, every single day. Are you aware of this?

We usually have a better attitude about choices that we make consciously. Unconscious decisions, on the other hand, lead to negative attitudes. Behaviors are both a person's greatest asset and their biggest block. According to Daniel Kahneman, the brain has two separate operating systems that affect attention. In his book *Thinking, Fast and Slow*, Kahneman calls these system 1 and system 2.

System 1 (Automatic System)	System 2 (Reflective System)
Effortless, subconscious, skill, associative, fast	Abstract, rule-based, aware, deductive
Eyeball estimate, framing prejudices	Evaluates options, makes conscious choices
Individuals	Economy

System 1 is involuntary. It recognizes the stimulus and executes. This system makes automatic decisions. Examples of this system could be the fact that a person turns their head when their name is called or recoils at the sight of a spider.

System 2, on the other hand, manages the will. It responds to the suggestions made by system 1, makes the final decision, and determines where it needs to focus its attention. The funny thing is that people assume all of their decisions are made consciously by system 2. In fact, the automatic reactions arising from system 1 are at play in every decision that is made. The following is an explanatory illustration of these two systems.

System 2 is responsible for everything arising from the will and self-control, and everything is exceedingly difficult for system 1. When making conscious decisions, it helps to realize that system 1 is always involved.

The perspective that we have on events plays a huge role when making conscious decisions. As Tony Robbins explains in his book

Awaken the Giant Within, everyone has a system or a process they use in every situation in life to determine what events mean to them and what must be done. Everyone has a different take on what happens depending on their perspective. The first thing that affects all of our assessments is our mental and emotional state when we make the assessment. The goal, of course, is to take advantage of every situation in life so that we always get the results that we want. A person can take the rudder and control their own processes of assessment.

We are what we think about. Whatever we are is born of our thoughts. With our thoughts we create our world.—Buddha

Perceptions are creative. There are many ways to interpret an experience. The brain tends to frame objects according to past perception. Reframing turns a negative expression into a positive one by changing the frame of reference used to perceive the experience. People can create more options in life by changing the way they perceive things. Behavior and understanding change. The brain sets to work creating a new situation.

The team creates the emotional atmosphere that it needs by making conscious decisions and taking responsibility for these decisions as it moves toward its goal.

This is a dynamic process. Depending on the needs that arise, the team will find it necessary to swap responsibilities and make new decisions. It is easier for a team to reach its goals if it consists of people who are capable of looking at things from different perspectives and who can express these ideas.

Team members can take advantage of archetypes in order to make conscious decisions after examining an issue from different perspectives. When the archetypes that guide unconscious (automatic) behaviors are selected and employed consciously, how one looks at events is naturally transformed.

The concept of an archetype first emerged in ancient Greece during the time of Plato and was later grafted into the world of modern psychology by Carl Jung.

Most of the archetypes on which this theory is based emerged from historical experience. Archetypes are elements of the collective unconscious. According to Jung, the collective unconscious is passed down to every person and largely consists of archetypes and mythology. When these archetypes become part of our own unconscious, they become personalized. Archetypes are an expression of the behaviors people engage in instinctively.

Basically, every person has 12 archetypes, which are the foundation on which a person's emotions, actions, impulses, and personality motivations are constructed. Archetypes that may create problems in terms of team dynamics and the behaviors they represent are provided below.

Little Parent. A child that takes the place of a parent. A small parent is a parent to other children and even to their own parents. These people bear a heavy internal burden because of the responsibilities they assume. Team members with this archetype are extremely protective, possessive, and take responsibility.

Mascot. The archetype of the fun-loving child. They are afraid of conflict within the family. They try to prevent conflict with humor and jokes. In order to avoid conflict, they prefer not making emotional connections. Team members with this archetype may prefer to adapt to the team rather than defend their own ideas.

Scapegoat. A problem child who has internalized family conflict. They were blamed for issues beyond their control when they were children. The result can be the development of an aggressive personality. They feel like they are the scapegoat, trapped and without hope. They constantly feel like something is wrong with them. Team members with this archetype may have issues with self-confidence, despair, and aggressive behavior.

Lost child. These lost children are forgotten and abandon their place. They withdraw into their own world through things like TV, games, and books. They feel unhappy and alone because they feel invisible in the family. They can become alienated from their family as adults. They tend to live in their own world. Team members with this archetype may build walls, remain aloof from team discussions, and have problems getting along.

Clever planner. The shrewd and opportunistic child. They are the type of children that adults are always trying to calm down and direct. They shrewdly observe the weaknesses in others, looking for opportunities to reach their goal. As adults, they have a habit of constantly labeling others and exhibit narcissistic behavior that poses a danger to their personal relationships. Team members with this archetype may have trouble adapting and try to find the weaknesses in others and leverage them to their own advantage as well as seeking a place of prominence.

Hero. We can see this person first discover their strength in their own life and then overcome obstacles and take risks to serve others. This archetype is associated with facing one's fears, becoming stronger through the confrontation, and embarking on a journey to personal autonomy. Those with this archetype frequently take personal and financial risks. They dare to take on matters that have dangerous consequences and they strive for victory. Team members with this archetype have the courage to take whatever risk is required to be a hero and lead the way. Because they are focused on success and locked on the target, they may not notice their own needs or those of the people around them.

ACTIVITY

Archetype Wheel

Purpose: For the team to experience what it means to take responsibility and improve their observational skills.

Duration: 30 minutes.

Materials: Symbols and descriptions of the archetypes, adhesive tape for making a wheel, paper, and pens.

First, all of the participants will walk around the wheel to get familiar with it. They will share their ideas about each part. Then, everyone will choose a partner. A and B will say which archetype they might be. They choose the archetype that they would least like to see in themselves and others when trying to achieve goals as a team. They will take the symbol that represents the archetype they chose and pin it on their lapel. They will identify which responsibility they will assume to prevent the behavior displayed by this archetype when it occurs and write down their pledge.

For example: "When I recognize the mascot's presence on the team, I will ask questions so that they can express what they are really thinking."

Group sharing: Everyone will share with the group what they noticed in the pair work and seek to answer the following questions.

1. Which archetypes are most prevalent on the team?
2. What could be a positive side to this archetype? How can you use this on the team?
3. What kind of team do you plan on becoming and which archetypes make it difficult for you to achieve this goal?
4. When you see these archetypes, who will be responsible for what?

Teamwork with Planets

Astronomers have, for many years, been studying the sun and our solar system, which includes the planets orbiting the sun. People have also studied the interaction between the solar system and humans, which are in and of themselves a system. They observed that different planets had different characteristics, which triggered different impulses in the human system. As with the archetypes, it is possible to connect the planets with the messages they communicate and the behaviors they represent.

Sun

Message: Whatever you do, put your creativity on display and express yourself! The impulses it represents are self-expression, creativity, and strength.

Mercury

Message: Whatever you do, define it, categorize it, and contemplate it! The impulses it represents are logical analysis, discussion of ideas, and communication.

Venus

Message: Whatever you do, do it in cooperation with others and enjoy it! The impulses it represents are aesthetics, pleasure, forming social relationships, politeness, and harmony.

Moon

Message: Whatever you do, pay attention to how it makes you feel! The impulses it represents are nurturing, sharing, and emotional bonding.

Mars

Message: You can do it. Get a move on! The impulses it represents are taking initiative, motivation, taking action, courage and resolve.

Jupiter

Message: Whatever you do, be fair and don't forget your values! The impulses it represents are fairness, optimism, and improvement.

Saturn

Message: Whatever you do, be disciplined and do not be slack in your work! The impulses it represents are being disciplined, durable, hardworking, and responsible.

Uranus

Message: Whatever you do, be original, unbiased, and non-judgmental! The impulses it represents are being unusual, working for the good of the whole, and not being prejudiced.

Neptune

Message: Whatever you do, you cannot control everything; sometimes you have to surrender! The impulses it represents are self-sacrifice and the ability to read and accept the emotional landscape.

Pluto

Message: Whatever you do, recognize the risks, but do not be afraid to take them if necessary! The impulses it represents are openness to change and transformation, the ability to take responsibility and lead on one's own.

ACTIVITY

Wheel of Planets

Purpose: To discover different kinds of energy and take responsibility for conveying that energy to the team.

Duration: 45 minutes.

Materials: Symbols of the planets, material for a collage (e.g. various images and magazines), scissors, glue, poster board, and tape to make a wheel.

First, all of the participants will walk around the wheel of planets to get familiar with it. They will share their ideas about each part. On the second time around, they are asked to stand by the planet that represents where they see themselves on the team right now. People who end up on the same planet will explain to their colleagues why they are there. Later, the whole group will share what they have recognized, and the leaders will make notes on the poster board. On the third time around, the participants will position themselves on the planets that they feel will help the team achieve its goals and where they feel there is a deficiency. Those who end up on the same planet will share their ideas. Later, the entire group will decide what planet's energy they will use.

Collage exercise: The new awareness gained from the archetype and planet exercises will be reinforced by making a collage. Cards with different emotions will be passed out and those that symbolize behaviors that are either needed or should be avoided will be chosen. Then, a collage will be made, and the team will craft a written commitment.

Team Coaching Skills: Obstacles to Team Success and Recognizing Support

have already referred to my work with Ms. Ayesha, who had been an executive in a technology company for six years. When she communicated the results of observations she made in a team meeting, one of the things she noted was that they were focused more on resources than on obstacles.

While I was doing research in preparation for my role as a panelist in Barcelona in October 2015 at the 17th Leadership Conference organized by the ILA (International Leadership Association), a respected international association, it was truly eye-opening for me to see the distribution of strengths and weaknesses that executives focus on in their employees. Research indicates that executives in the US focus on strengths 41% of the time and areas for improvement 59% of the time when giving feedback to their employees. In the UK, 38% of the feedback is on strengths and 62% on areas of improvement. But as you go east, the difference widens in favor of areas of improvement, so that in China and Japan, it is 24% on strengths and 76% on areas of improvement.

It is only natural to anticipate a similar trend for strengths and areas of improvement when the issue is a team and not the individual. Obviously, in both areas, there are factors arising either from individuals or the systems they find themselves in. With this awareness, it is important that we clearly identify obstacles and activate our strategies for overcoming them. However, another issue that is just as important is our ability to identify the resources at our disposal and how we can activate them for the optimal good of the team and turn them into action.

Perception creates reality. When beliefs become an obsession, they become rigid, unchangeable, and oppressive. We must not reject the truth that letting go of beliefs and becoming free is an option.

When a person looks in the mirror, they will see various internal agreements. These agreements were created by family, school, culture, friends, etc. They are the answers given to the question "Who am I?" These answers are the acknowledgments and agreements that conditions create for the individual. Thoughts communicate belief systems and loyalties.

The more powerful the beliefs are, the harder it is for a person to recognize their true self, because the true self is hidden behind the belief systems. Don Miguel Ruiz Jr. explains how the true self hides in his book *The Five Levels of Attachment* using the smokey mirror analogy. According to him, smoke prevents a person from seeing their true self.

People invest in themselves for a story they want to believe. They strive to create their own persona (masks) in order to be "someone." Once a person accepts that they are perfect just as they are, all their attachments, internal criticism, and conflict come to an end. The most important step in this process is a person accepting and loving themselves. "I accept myself as I am." The person who can say this begins to develop and evolve with life.

According to author and researcher Professor Brené Brown, the general consensus in society is that a person is perceived as weak if they show that they are sensitive and fragile. As a result, everyone wears a mask of some kind to avoid appearing weak as part of their effort to hide how fragile they are. When relationships develop trust, people can bravely leave their comfort zones and reveal their brokenness to others. Then, they don't have to wear a mask anymore.

Mask Exercise

Purpose: To raise awareness on the team about different beliefs and identities.

Duration: 45 minutes.

Materials: Blank masks, colorful markers, decorative materials, glue

Work in groups of five. Everyone is given ten minutes to make a mask. Blank masks and materials to color them are provided to the group. Everyone prepares the mask that they wear most frequently and presents it to the rest of the group. Each participant is given five minutes for discussion. The team will ask the person who presents the following questions:

- What do you become when you put this mask on?
- What are you hiding behind this mask?
- In what area of your life do you most often use this mask?
- What are the advantages?
- If you were to take off the mask and throw it away, what would be different?

Follow-up questions:

- How does the team see this person with the mask?
- How does the team want to see this person?
- What are the advantages and disadvantages of this mask for the team?

The group listens to the answers to these questions and gives feedback to the speaker. Take turns until everyone has explained their mask.

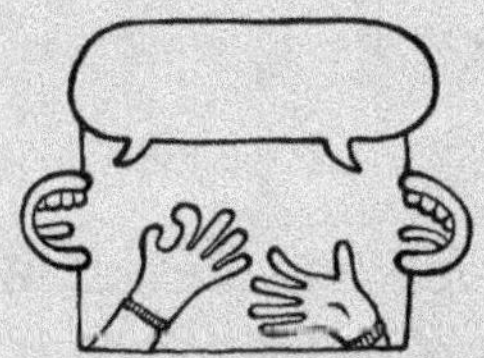

Discussion Time

Take time to share thoughts regarding personal masks. The entire group will speak and discuss the mask they wear for the outside world as a team. How does this mask protect the team? What do they want to change?

Obstacles to Achieving Team Goals: Shadows

The shadow side includes all of the things that a person tries to hide or deny. It is the person that they choose not to be. It includes all of the sinister aspects that are unacceptable to their family, their social circle, and themselves. For example, violence, temper, hostility, concern, etc.

The shadow side is the hidden version of the person that is deeply buried. The message is noticeably clear: "There is something wrong with me. I am not acceptable. I am not lovable."

The shadow side manifests when it is reflected to others. Therefore, when a person achieves balance in their personal world, this effect will be reflected to their environment.

The shadow side is not only an expression of negativity. It is a concept that represents whatever is not brought into the light of conscious awareness. No matter how deeply a person buries them, shadows will find their way to the light of day because they are part of who the person is.

A light that leads to success will shine only when we have the courage to confront everything as it really is without deceiving or lying to ourselves. —I Ching

People bury a trait because they cannot live with it. They resist looking at it or examining it for any length of time. Robert Bly describes the shadow as "a long bag we drag behind us." He says, "We spend our life until we're twenty deciding what parts of ourselves to put in the bag, and we spend the rest of our lives trying to get them out again."

A person begins to narrow their frame of reference due to the shadow while trying to keep the unwanted traits out of their life. What is left creates a deficient personality that is not a complete reflection of the person, as it includes only the traits they like. Jung calls this masked personality "Persona." Persona and shadow exist within the individual as two opposing elements.

When people recognize their dark side, they instinctively ignore it, or they begin to negotiate with it. Embracing the shadow frees us from the destructive and obstructive aspects of the shadow and releases the life energy that has been restrained by the masks worn to hide the traits viewed as unacceptable. When the shadow is accepted and embraced, a person no longer has to be afraid and appear to be something they are not. Otherwise, a person becomes owned by something that is not possessed, and what they resist persistently continues to exist.

I swear by God that when you see your own beauty, you will worship yourself.
—Mevlâna Celâleddin-i Rûmî

All of the so-called mistakes, and everything a person hates about themselves, are actually their most valuable traits. They have only been blown out of proportion. It is like any instrument in an orchestra being too loud and disrupting the harmony of the music.

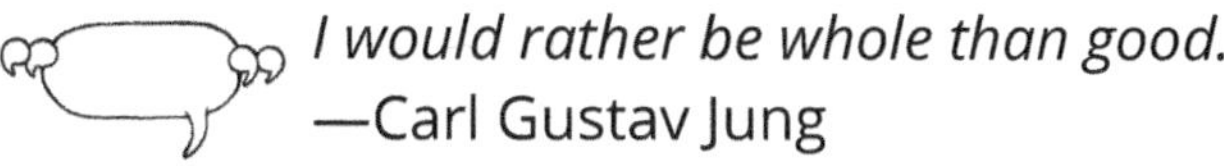

I would rather be whole than good.
—Carl Gustav Jung

Jung said that people can find enlightenment by shaping the darkness, not by envisioning figures of light. To achieve psychological wholeness, a person should not suppress characteristics they don't like, but rather find the positive side of these traits and accept them.

According to Jung, everything tends to become its opposite. He argues that a dimension that is overly suppressed in one's personality can turn into something that is the exact opposite. Coming to terms with the dark side prevents this from happening.

We can only transform the traits we dislike in ourselves and others by observing and accepting them.—Ken Wilber

The purpose of the shadow exercise is to become whole, end the suffering, and stop playing hide-and-seek with ourselves. Ignoring the massive elephant walking around the room will only end with you being crushed by the elephant at some point. A person who accepts their dark side improves the quality of their personality. In addition, we gain greater insight and begin to be less afraid of the external representations of our shadow.

ACTIVITY

Shadow Exercise

Purpose: Increased awareness of the shadow behaviors of team members and the team.

Duration: 20 minutes.

Materials: Paper and pens.

Paired exercise. A will ask B to think of a person they cannot stand and jot down three traits they don't like about this person. After two minutes, B will jot down two more traits that this person has.

A will ask B the following questions:

- What percentage of these do you have and in what areas of your life do you experience them?
- How do you reflect these behaviors?

Later, A will give feedback about how he/she has observed these behaviors in B. After five minutes of discussion, A and B will switch places.

When that is finished, A and B will spend three minutes discussing the shadow behavior they see on the team and choose one of their observations to share with the group.

Discussion Time

Discuss what undesirable traits the participants observed in themselves and what new awareness has resulted from this. Share shadow behaviors observed in the group.

Obstacles to Achieving Team Goals: Snipers

Everyone has the Sniper, who represents the voices that suddenly shoot a person down when they are trying to make progress. This is Jung's saboteur archetype. In order to understand its positive traits, people must confront their internal Sniper. The Sniper is especially active during times of change and warns a person about the risks they may face if they leave their comfort zone. Although the effect may be beneficial as long as the warning goes no further than worry, when it rises to the level of fear, the Sniper has the power to throw a person off track. When a person makes a decision but then changes their mind due to fear or when they turn back with excuses after embarking on a journey to complete a task, it shows that the Sniper is in control. The weapon used by the Sniper is fear, wielding it to sabotage the person.

One of the positive aspects of this archetype is that the person sees the obstacles that block their way, which ensures that they don't repeat the same mistakes. At this point, the excuses end, and the pursuit of desires begins. A person can ask themselves the following questions to see the Sniper's power:

- What fears do I have?
- What fear is preventing me from achieving my purpose?
- Am I pursuing my desires or am I finding excuses and putting them off?
- Am I aware that I am shooting myself down?
- Do I easily accept praise and compliments, or does it make me uncomfortable to hear them?

There are one or more voices in everyone's head that hold them back. These voices have one mission—to protect the status quo. The bigger the dream or step to be taken, the fiercer the battle waged by the Sniper.

This Sniper could be described as the internal opposition, the negative inner voice, and it always has a reason why the plan won't work. The reason will be shaped differently depending on the coachee. The reason could be that the plan is stupid, dangerous, hopeless, etc.

These voices generally cling to some small bit of truth and try to thwart the plan so that it never gets off the ground. By getting in touch with their strengths and discovering their strong inner voices, people can create a shield to protect themselves from the Sniper.

The emotional atmosphere created on the team affects everyone, especially their motivation, so the Team Coach must be aware of Snipers and help the team recognize them when they appear. If the team recognizes the strengths (contributions) of a Sniper, this creates a protective shield for the team while using the benefits of the Sniper.

 *You can always cope with now, but you can never cope with the future, nor do you have to...*
—Eckhart Tolle

I ♥
Sabot

Snipers

Purpose: To gain awareness of the obstructive voices on the path to achieving your goals.

Duration: 25 minutes.

Materials: Paper and pens.

Paired exercise. For five minutes, A will describe to B the voices they hear from the Sniper within her/himself.

- In what situations do you hear these voices? What do they say?
- What is the Sniper like?
- What fears or shadows in A does the Sniper take advantage of?
- B will then spend three minutes giving A feedback about the voices they observe in A.
- A and B will swap places.

For five minutes, they will talk about the Snipers they observed in themselves and choose two conclusions to share with the group.

Group exercise: All of the team members will share which Snipers they have observed. A joint statement will be formulated by the team about its collective Sniper. They will reach a consensus about how to recognize the Sniper and what they will do about it. The team will share their insights into what is possible and not possible on the team when there is no Sniper.

Support in Achieving Team Goals: Sage

Jung's Sage archetype is expressed as a polite, wise, compassionate father figure. This Sage has profound experience in all matters, and views everything that happens as experience in order to focus on the lessons that need to be learned. Sages appreciate the lesson underlying every experience. They are mentors that can show people who they are right now and what they can achieve if they want to. They gently and calmly hold their hand as they move toward their goals, showing them how to achieve their full potential.

Conversing With Your Inner Sage

Purpose: To create awareness of supportive mechanisms on the way to achieving goals.

Duration: 15 minutes.

Materials: Paper and pens.

Paired exercise. For 5 minutes, A will describe to B their own Sage.

- What benefits can this Sage bring to their life?
- What is the word they use most frequently?
- What kind of contribution can they make to the team?

A and B will swap places. For five minutes, they will discuss the characteristics and benefits of the team's Sage. Two benefits will be chosen to share with the group.

Group exercise: All of the team members will discuss the profile of the Sage they would like to have on the team. They will identify a joint slogan/name and mode of operation for the team Sage. They will discuss how the Sage will be called and how to take advantage of the Sage's assistance when it is needed.

60+ / 40 - 60 / 30
9 months / 10 / 20

ACTIVITY

Steps And Support

Purpose: To help members of the team recognize their own strengths and identify the team's strengths.

Duration: 30 minutes.

Materials: Symbols that represent life stages, note paper and pens.

Group exercise: All participants.

Review the life stages introduced in the section on Building Trust (p. 100). Create a representative road map in which every life stage is considered a separate stop. The following questions will be answered for each life stage. A strength recognized at each stop will be jotted down.

At the end of the activity, the participants will be given five minutes to make a list of their own strengths. These lists will later be shared with the group.

1. **Stage—First 9 months: Mother's Womb**
   Fundamental outcome: Hope, trust, dependence
   * How can you benefit from this stage in your life right now? How would this benefit affect the team?

2. **Stage—Up until the age of 10: Childhood**
   Fundamental outcome: Curiosity, courage, desire to experience
   * What gifts will this child give you? How will this be reflected on the team?

3. **Stage—Up until the age of 20: Adolescence**
   Fundamental outcome: Freedom, boldly defending their own truth, open to new experiences, rebels against rules, adventurous, desire to develop and prepare themselves.

- What does the adolescent inside of you want? How does the team benefit?

4. Stage—Up until the age of 30: Young Adult
Fundamental outcome: Love, sharing, trust, the ability to stand on their own.
- How can the young adult support you today? How do you support the team today as a young adult?

5. Stage—Ages 30–60: Mature Adult
Fundamental outcome: Vision phase, desire to make their work valuable, making decisions based on the direction life is taking.
- What steps could you take to make your life more valuable? How can you add value to the team?

6. Stage—Ages 60+: Old Age
Fundamental outcome: Wisdom, acceptance, appreciating what is, a holistic perspective.
- How can your inner Sage contribute to the team?

I ♥ sabotage

ACTIVITY

Awareness Exercise: Smokey Mirror

Purpose: To review everything that has been learned and draw up team agreements for the future.

Duration: 20 minutes.

Materials: Mirror, paper, pens.

The entire team will stand in front of a large smoky mirror. They will ask the mirror the following questions:

- Mirror, mirror, on the wall, tell us what we need to get rid of this smoke?
- What masks do we need to remove?
- Which of our shadows should we accept?
- Which obstructive voices should we listen to?
- What should we leave in the past? What should we let go of?

As the things left in the past emerge, the mirror's smoke will begin to lift, and in the end the mirror will be clear and clean.

The team will ask the mirror the following:

- Mirror, mirror on the wall, tell us what this team has become.
- What is possible from this point forward?
- What are the team's greatest strengths when it comes to achieving this goal?

Discussion Time

Sharing the experiences gained throughout the training and sharing emotions to achieve closure of the process.

Conclusion

During the last 17 years in the field of leadership and team development as a coach, I recognized that there was an enormous need for an integrated and holistic view for individuals as well as teams in every moment and situation. This book was written to support you to have the best of both worlds in a unique, authentic way while being easily aware of multiple views in any given moment, space, and conditions.

The goal of *Better Leaders, Better Teams* is to expand the field of view of teams and leaders. This approach aims to provide a look into interior factors and external performance indicators while considering how each person exists in the "We" and how it's affected by the system it exists in.

It's not just "We." It's I, it's you, it's us, it's all of us.

It also gives a voice to the system we're living in. As a leader, you need to consider the team and all the individuals within the team, their performance, plus the system they find themselves in, which often goes unnoticed.

So, a leader's main objective is to have a bird's-eye view of these domains and create a vision, an inclusive vision, for all of them. If the leader ignores any of these domains or makes decisions from their dominant perspective, they will create blind spots that will prevent them from seeing the big picture. This limited vision will create problems which they'll continuously be forced to solve. Having the skillset to see the shadows and recognize the snipers, which are usually seen as obstacles to success, will allow the coach to turn them into weapons for success.

Every single living organism's basic instinct is to survive, whether it's a team, organization, or a country. People's behaviors are mostly the result of their survival mechanisms. There's no such thing as a right or wrong mechanism. Rather than judging them, we need to find how we can utilize them for progress. As a leader, using the tools of a coach and having a holistic perspective, you can easily understand yourself, your team, and your organization.

To summarize, *Better Leaders, Better Teams* provides you with an opportunity to see things holistically. This is a crucial skill in order to thrive during chaotic times, a point that has been made clear during various crises.

"There Is Nothing New Under the Sun!"

Well, you have come to the end of the book, and I congratulate you for your dedication. As an adult who is all too aware of the fact that I have not been able to resolve every issue I have faced, I realize that you may not be able to resolve every issue you face either. That is probably what it means to be human—the art of being able to respond to whatever life throws at you with the resources at your disposal.

Our collective journey as reader and author began with the importance of drawing up team agreements and taking joint responsibility, and continued with a study of the elements, where we emphasized how the differences between individuals can be transformed into advantages. We have focused on team coaching skills to draw your attention to the importance of listening, asking powerful questions, and improving communication skills. Archetypes and the personalities of the planets have been used to create common goals. We have discussed shadows, snipers, and your inner sage. We have drawn upon the fundamental aspects of your life journey and considered how all of these insights can be conveyed to the team. Team coaching skills have been augmented with numerous and varied activities.

I've had the privilege to be a student of great teachers, such as Ken Wilber, John Carter, Philip Sandler, Janet Harvey, Julio Olalla, Jan Jacob Stam, Dorothy Siminovitch, Bilge Şeker, Mehmet Zararsızoğlu, Sun Woo, Ji Woo, Tolga Olgun, and Avi Goren-Bar, to name a few. They all impacted my life journey deeply, and I'm so grateful for every contribution they made.

I'm also grateful to my dear mentor and colleague Kimberly Hunn for the time she spent reading this book's draft and the valuable comments she made that improved the content.

I also thank Said Tekin for his creative illustrations that brought lightness to serious matters and Volkan Dalyan for his extraordinary work on the cover, as well as Zeynep Balcı for her element test, which gave a natural touch to this book.

Finally, to my dear friend and colleague Bethany Kelly of Publishing Partner. Without your support I would not have made it across the finish line. I deeply admire your dedication, your flexibility and understanding, and your ability to utilize your resources whenever needed.

I took advantage of numerous sources in the preparation of this book, sifting information and adding my own experience from my corporate career as well as my coaching career.

It is my sincere hope that the things shared in this book will be valuable both to you and the teams that you are working with or will work with, providing alternatives you can employ to handle whatever life brings your way.

A final quotation comes from John A. Shed: "A ship in harbor is safe, but that is not what ships are built for." Life is unpredictable, and every corner might include some challenges that help us to grow. What I've learned so far is to stay fit psychologically, physically, emotionally, and mentally. This is only possible if we can establish supporting resources and structures. To support people around me on multiple levels, I need to support myself on multiple levels.

It is my hope that you will meet more frequently with the real "YOU" behind the smoke in your mirrors and share this person more often with the people you interact with.

With affection and gratitude,
Sami Bugay

Me

What I will continue to do

Me

What I will stop doing

Me

What I will change about myself

Team

What we will continue to do

____

____

____

____

____

____

____

____

____

____

____

____

____

Team

What we will stop doing

Team

What we will change about our team

About the Author

When he was introduced to coaching in 2002, Sami Bugay experienced and witnessed the positive effects firsthand, which inspired him to take part in the first coaching training sessions offered in Turkey.

He not only has over 7,000 hours of coaching experience, but he also holds the following accreditations: Master Certified Coach MCC-ICF, Registered ICF Mentor Coach, NCC - Certified Ontological Coach and ICF PCC Assessor. In 2009, he served as the Turkey Vice President of the International Coaching Federation (ICF). Bugay brought ICF Turkey together with Endeavor, which supports global entrepreneurship. He won the "Local Spirit, Global Presence" award at the ICF 2008 Conference in Montreal for his project called, "Turkey's Coaches Support Turkish Entrepreneurship."

As the founder and managing director of KA Consultancy, Bugay serves both individuals and leading domestic and international companies in Turkey and abroad in the area of Leadership and Team Development. Sami Bugay has extensive experience in different positions of senior management, which is a distinct advantage in the coaching process.

Bugay served as the International Coach Federation Turkey President in the 2016-2018 term and is the founder and head teacher at Integral Coaching™ ACTP-ICF.

General Bibliography

Allamby, David. *The Manager's Coaching Toolkit*. London: Pearson Education, 2006.

Brown, Brené. *Daring Greatly*. New York: Penguin, 2012.

Carnegie, Dale. *Etkin Takım* Çalışması. İstanbul, 2008.

Clutterbuck, David. *Coaching the Team at Work*. Nicholas Brealey Publishing, 2007.

Corporate Coach Articles. Brefi Group Limited, 2013.

Donnellon, Anne. *Leading Teams*. Boston: Harvard Business School Press, 2002.

Ford, Debbie. *Işığı Arayanların Karanlık Yanı*. Akaşa. Istanbul, 2011.

Forrest, Steven. İçinizdeki *Gökyüzü*. Barış İlhan Yayınevi. 1997.

Froh, Jeffrey J., and Acacia C. Parks. *Activities for Teaching Positive Psychology*. Washington, DC: American Psychological Association, 2013.

Gladwell, Malcolm. *Blink: The Power of Thinking without Thinking*. New York: Penguin Books, 2006.

Goleman, Daniel. *Focus*. New York: Harper Collins, 2014.

Goleman, Daniel. *Sosyal Zeka*. Varlık Yayınları. Istanbul, 2007.

Goleman, Daniel, R. Boyatzis, and A. McKee. *Primal Leadership*. Boston: Harvard Business Review Press, 2013.

Goleman, Daniel, R. Boyatzis, and A. McKee. *Yeni Liderler*. Varlık Yayınları. Istanbul, 2012.

Gottman, John, and Nan Silver. *Evliliği Sürdürmenin Yedi* İlkesi Varlık Yayınları. 2013.

Hawkins, John. *What Exactly Does Ethical Leadership Mean These Days?* Community Links, 7 (3), 3, 10. Leadership Edge, 2000.

Jones, Alanna. *Team-Building Activities for Every Group*. Rec Room Publishing, 1999.

Jones, Laurie Beth. *The Four Elements of Success*. Nashville: Thomas Nelson, 2005

Kahneman, Daniel. *Thinking, Fast and Slow*. New York: Farrar, Straus and Giroux, 2013.

Katzenbach, Jon R., and Douglas K. Smith. *The Wisdom of Teams: Creating the High-Performance Organization*. McKinsey & Company, 1993.

Kim, Peter H., D. L. Ferrin, C. D. Cooper, and K. T. Dirks. "Removing the Shadow of Suspicion: The Effects of Apology Versus Denial for Repairing Competence-Versus Integrity-Based Trust Violations." *Journal of Applied Psychology* 89 (2004): 104–118.

Kouzes, James M., and Barry Z. Posner. *The Leadership Challenge*. San Francisco: Jossey-Bass, 2003.

Lazare, Aaron. *On Apology*. New York: Oxford University Press, 2004.

Lencioni, Patrick. *İş Dünyasında Koçlar ve Mentorlar*. Türkiye İş Bankası Yayınları. 2003.

Luecke, Richard. *Bir Ekip Yaratmak*. Translated by Sedat Büyükarslan. İş Bankası Kültür Yayınları. Istanbul, 2008.

Martin, Curly. *The Business Coaching Handbook*. Crown House Publishing, 2007.

Mashihi, Sandra, and Kenneth Nowack. *Clueless: Coaching People Who Just Don't Get It*. Envisia Learning, 2011.

Maxwell, John C. *Developing the Leader Within You*. Nashville: Thomas Nelson, 1993.

Meese, Edwin, and P. J. Ortmeier. *Leadership, Ethics, and Policing: Challenges for the 21st Century*. Prentice Hall, 2004.

Miller, Brian Cole. *Quick Team-Building Activities for Busy Managers*. Amacom, 2004.

Mindell, Amy. *Metaskills: The Spiritual Art of Therapy*. New Falcon Publications, 1995.

Musashi, Miyamoto. *The Book of Five Rings*. Aristeus Books, 2012.

Newstrom, John, and Edward Scannell. *The Big Book of Team-Building Games*. New York: McGraw-Hill, 1998.

Palmer, Wendy, and Janet Crawford. *Leadership Embodiment*. CreateSpace, 2013.

Pink, Daniel H. *Drive*. Canongate, 2009.

Richardson, Linda. *Sales Coaching*. 2nd ed. New York: McGraw-Hill, 2009.

Robbins, Anthony. İçindeki *Devi Uyandır*. İnkılap Kitabevi. Istanbul, 2003.

Rosen, Keith. *Coaching Salespeople Into Sales Champions*. Wiley & Sons, 2008.

Rosenberg, Marshall B. Şiddetsiz İletişim. Remzi Kitabevi. Istanbul, 2011.

Ruiz, don Miguel, Jr. *The Five Levels of Attachment*. London: Hay House, 2013.

Scannell, Mary, and Edward E. Scannell. *The Big Book of Team Motivating Games*. New York: McGraw-Hill, 2010.

Schiffman, Stephan. *The #1 Sales Team*. Adams Media, 2006.

Schlenker, Barry R. "Aberrant Images." Chap. 10 in *Impression Management: The Self-Concept, Social Identity, and Interpersonal Relations*, 285–303. Monterey: Brooks/Cole, 1980.

Tamblyn, Doni, and Sharyn Weiss. *The Big Book of Humorous Training Games*. New York: McGraw-Hill, 2000.

Tolle, Eckhart. *The Power of Now*. Namaste Publishing, 1997.

Tucker, Sean, N. Turner, J. Barling, E. M. Reid, and C. Elving. "Apologies and Transformational Leadership." *Journal of Business Ethics* 63, no. 2 (2006): 195–207.

Whitworth, Laura, Karen Kimsey-House, H. Kimsey-House, and P. Sandahl. *Co-Active Coaching*. 2nd ed. Davies-Black Publishing, 2007.

Whitworth, Laura, Karen Kimsey-House, H. Kimsey-House, and P. Sandahl. *Koaktif Koçluk*. Media Cat, 2008.

Wilber, Ken. *A Brief History of Everything*. Boulder, CO: Shambhala Press, 2007.

Wilber, Ken. *The Integral Approach*. Boulder, CO: Shambhala Press, n.d.

Zeus, Perry, and Suzanne Skiffington. *The Complete Guide to Coaching at Work*. New York: McGraw-Hill, 2004.

Internet Sources

Please note that that Internet links listed may have changed or disappeared between when this work was written and when it is read.

Brown, Brené. *The Power of Vulnerability*. TEDxHouston, June 2010. http://www.ted.com/talks/brene_brown_on_vulnerability

Co-Active Training Institute. http://www.thecoaches.com/

Cooper, Belle Beth. "The Two Brain Systems that Control Our Attention: The Science of Gaining Focus." Buffer (blog). February 8, 2014. http://blog.bufferapp.com/the-science-of-focus-and-how-to-improve-your-attention-span

Encyclopedia Britannica Online. s.v. "Gestalt psychology." Accessed January 22, 2021. http://global.britannica.com/EBchecked/topic/232098/Gestalt-psychology

Mind Tools. "What Are Your Values? Deciding What's Most Important in Life." Accessed January 22, 2012. http://www.mindtools.com/pages/article/newTED_85.htm

Keating, Steve. "Your Attitude Is Your Choice." Lead Today (blog). July 20, 2012. http://stevekeating.me/2012/07/20/your-attitude-is-your-choice/

Paradigm Partnership Ltd. http://www.paradigm-partnership.co.uk/

Pritchard, Mary E. "Doing vs. Being." *Huffington Post*. Updated December 23, 2013. http://www.huffingtonpost.com/mary-pritchard/doing-being_b_4144965.html

Reference, "What Is the Difference Between Values and Beliefs?" Last updated April 10, 2020. http://www.ask.com/question/what-is-the-meaning-of-personal-values

Robbins, Mike. "The Power of Appreciation." Accessed January 22, 2021. http://mike-robbins.com/the-power-of-appreciation/

Timson, Judith. "The Sorry State of Apology." *The Globe and Mail*. March 19, 2003. https://www.theglobeandmail.com/report-on-business/the-sorry-state-of-apology/article18284766/

http://www.bernaozcandemir.com/bilincalti-konulari/arketipler

http://www.bilgiustam.com/psikososyal-gelisim-kurami-ve-evre-leri/

http://www.kigem.com/etkin-dinleme-becerisini-kazanmak.html